SIEGES
THAT CHANGED
THE WORLD

ALAMO

CONSTANTINOPLE

DIEN BIEN PHU

MASADA

PETERSBURG

STALINGRAD

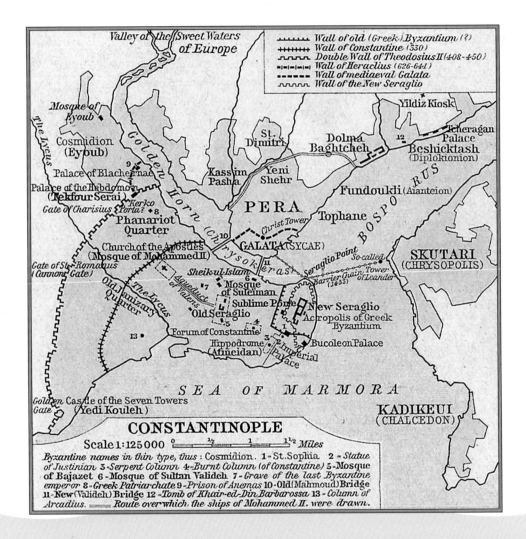

Valley of the Sweet Waters
of Europe

	Wall of old (Greek) Byzantium (?)
	Wall of Constantine (330)
	Double Wall of Theodosius II (408-450)
	Wall of Heraclius (626-641)
	Wall of mediaeval Galata
	Wall of the New Seraglio

Mosque of
Eyoub

Yildiz Kiosk

The Lycus

Cosmidion
(Eyoub)

*St.
Dimitri*

Dolma
Baghtcheh

12

Tcheragan
Palace

Beshicktash
(Diplokionion)

Palace of Blachernae

Kassim
Pasha

Yeni
Shehr

9

Fundoukli (Aianteion)

Palace of the Hebdomon
(Tekfour Serai)

PERA

BOSPO
RUS

*Kerko
Porta?*

Gate of Charisius

8

Phanariot
Quarter

Christ Tower

Tophane

SKUTARI
(CHRYSOPOLIS)

Church of the Apostles
(Mosque of Mohammed II)

10

GALATA (SYCAE)

Chrysokeras

Seraglio Point

So-called

Gate of St. Romanus
(Cannon-Gate)

Sheikul Islam

*Barrier Chain
(1453)*

Tower of Leander

*Old Janizary
Quarter*

The Lycus

*Aqueduct
of Valens*

6

Mosque
of Suleiman

7

New Seraglio
Acropolis of Greek
Byzantium

Sublime Porte

Old Seraglio

5

4

13

Forum of Constantine

Bucoleon Palace

Hippodrome
(Atmeidan)

3

2

1

*Imperial
Palace*

SEA   OF   MARMORA

Golden
Gate

Castle of the Seven Towers
(Yedi Kouleh)

KADIKEUI
(CHALCEDON)

CONSTANTINOPLE

Scale 1:125 000   0   ½   1   1½   Miles

Byzantine names in thin type, thus: Cosmidion. 1 - St. Sophia   2 - Statue
of Justinian 3 - Serpent Column 4 - Burnt Column (of Constantine) 5 - Mosque
of Bajazet 6 - Mosque of Sultan Valideh 7 - Grave of the last Byzantine
emperor 8 - Greek Patriarchate 9 - Prison of Anemas 10 - Old (Mahmoud) Bridge
11 - New (Valideh) Bridge 12 - Tomb of Khair-ed-Din Barbarossa 13 - Column of
Arcadius. ____ Route over which the ships of Mohammed II. were drawn.

CONSTANTINOPLE

TIM McNEESE

CHELSEA HOUSE
P U B L I S H E R S

A Haights Cross Communications Company

Philadelphia

FRONTIS This map of Constantinople has a legend showing when the walls around it were built down through the ages. The wall labeled as the Double Wall of Theodosius II was the one in place during the siege of 1453.

CHELSEA HOUSE PUBLISHERS

VP, NEW PRODUCT DEVELOPMENT Sally Cheney
DIRECTOR OF PRODUCTION Kim Shinners
CREATIVE MANAGER Takeshi Takahashi
MANUFACTURING MANAGER Diann Grasse

STAFF FOR CONSTANTINOPLE

EXECUTIVE EDITOR Lee Marcott
ASSOCIATE EDITOR Bill Conn
PRODUCTION EDITOR Jaimie Winkler
PICTURE RESEARCHER Pat Burns/Sarah Bloom
SERIES & COVER DESIGNER Keith Trego
LAYOUT 21st Century Publishing and Communications, Inc.

A Haights Cross Communications ⚊ Company

http://www.chelseahouse.com

First Printing

1 3 5 7 9 8 6 4 2

Library of Congress Cataloging-in-Publication Data

McNeese, Tim.
    The siege of Constantinople: April 6–May 29, 1453 / Tim McNeese.
        p. cm.—(Sieges that changed the world)
Summary: Describes the background to and the events of the 1453 siege of the Christian city of Constantinople, capital of the Byzantine Empire, by Turkish Muslims. Includes bibliographical references and index.
    ISBN 0-7910-7102-2 HC   0-7910-7527-3 PB
    1. Istanbul (Turkey)—History—Siege, 1453—Juvenile literature.
2. Sieges—Juvenile literature. [1. Istanbul (Turkey)—History—Siege, 1453.
2. Turkey—History—1288–1453.] I. Title. II. Series.
DF649 .M36 2002
949.5'04—dc21
                                                                2002015904

TABLE OF CONTENTS

1

The Empire of the East

For six horrific weeks, Turkish invaders had bombarded the besieged ancient city of Constantinople, capital of the Byzantine Empire. The year was 1453. The people of the city, who numbered 80,000, had endured a relentless barrage of granite cannonballs, some weighing as much as 1,200 pounds (544 kilograms), launched by huge Turkish siege cannons. As the days slipped by, the Byzantines watched as portions of their city walls crumbled into ruins. With each passing week, the threat of a Turkish victory seemed closer at hand.

On May 24, despite the constant prayers of the Christian city, ominous events occurred. This led the Byzantines to believe that God had turned his back on them. An ancient prophecy had promised that Constantinople would never fall when the moon was almost full. That night, however, during a full moon, a three-hour eclipse left the city in total darkness. The next day, as the people carried an image of the Virgin Mary through the city streets and prayed to her for protection, the religious icon fell to the ground. Then, a violent thunderstorm engulfed the region. Helpless children were washed down the city's streets. On the following day, a heavy fog engulfed Constantinople, a rare occurrence for the month of May. Three days later, the Turkish Muslims broke through the walls of the city, ending the siege. The last days of the Byzantine Empire had been filled with chaos, desperation, and bloodshed.

The collapse of Constantinople symbolized the end of Christian power in the part of Europe that had once been the eastern half of the Roman Empire. It also caused one of history's final links with the ancient world of the Greeks and the Romans to break.

How were the Turks able to bring about the final destruction of the ancient Byzantine Empire? What caused the collapse of this last remnant of the empire of the Caesars?

For over a thousand years, the Byzantine Empire stood in defiance of history. In the fifth century A.D., the Roman Empire, which had been a great power, was in shambles. Hundreds of years old, the empire found itself facing internal strife, being threatened by its own subjects. The imperial government of Rome had become corrupt and had lost touch with its old values. Invaders stood ready at the weakened empire's borders. The Romans watched as hordes of Germanic tribesmen swarmed across Rome's fortified borders, causing the collapse of the western portion of the empire.

Some Roman emperors had seen the invasion coming. In an effort to better defend the empire, Emperor Diocletian (who reigned A.D. 284–305) had divided the empire into two halves, each of which was ruled by two co-emperors. After the death of Diocletian, the empire experienced a power struggle. A new emperor, Constantine I, son of one of the co-emperors, emerged as the sole ruler of the empire. For his own protection, he moved the capital of the empire to the site of an ancient Greek city known as Byzantium, which was located in the east. In 330, he renamed the city Constantinople after himself and declared it the new center of Roman power. By the reign of Constantine, the city of Byzantium was already a thousand years old. Its next thousand years would prove even more splendid than the first.

By the next century, what had been the western half of the Roman Empire had fallen into ruin and chaos, as the Germanic tribes took former Roman territory for themselves. Marauding Germans repeatedly attacked the once-glorious center of the empire, the ancient city of Rome. Invaders from Asia, known as the Huns, also arrived and further devastated the city. As Rome experienced its final days of power, Constantinople became even more important as a center of Roman imperial power.

Constantinople's location was the key to its importance as a Roman city. Located on a slice of hill country, a land-mass easily defended in time of war, Constantinople stood at the mouth of the Bosporus, the channel of water that connects the Black Sea with the Sea of Marmara in what is now northwestern Turkey. An inlet of the Bosporus, called the Golden Horn, bordered the northeast portion of the city. The Sea of Marmara connects through a second narrow channel to the Aegean and Mediterranean seas. Ships sailing from the Mediterranean to the Black Sea were forced to pass through Constantinople, which gave the city the power to control the region's trade.

Built on seven hills, just as Rome had been, the city of Constantinople was a jewel. Because of its geographic location, it was destined to be a city of splendor and wealth. Constantine himself made certain of that before his death. He turned the ancient Greek city into a new center of art and learning. He ordered the construction of palaces, libraries, and museums. The emperor brought noble families from Italy to Constantinople and built fine mansions for them. Most of the architecture was patterned after Roman models.

Constantine also built a large chariot racetrack called the Hippodrome. It was much like the one located in Rome. The arena could seat more than 60,000 spectators. The Hippodrome not only hosted chariot races, but also featured mock animal hunts, bear fights, and occasionally, the execution of a dishonest public official. Later decades saw the building of large theaters, public and private baths, aqueducts to bring water to the city, and huge granaries. Visitors to Constantinople often commented on how much the city reminded them of the first capital of the Roman Empire: Rome itself.

Unlike Rome, though, a new form of building dotted the urban landscape of Constantinople. Because Constantine supported Christianity, he ordered the construction of great churches that were wonderfully decorated with marble, precious metals, and religious artwork. He began to build the greatest church in Byzantine history—the *Hagia Sophia*, or Church of the Divine Wisdom. His Church of the Holy Apostles, another of his great architectural wonders, included 13 tombs— a symbolic one for each of the 12 followers of Jesus, plus one for Constantine himself. Crosses were placed in public placces all around the city. Holy relics were purchased and brought to the city. Among Constantinople's relics were (or were believed to be) the bones of saints, such as St. Luke, St. Andrew, and St. Timothy; some of Noah's tools; and even the actual cross of Jesus, found by

Built by Constantine the Great and reconstructed by Emperor Justinian, the Hagia Sophia was a symbol of Constantinople's splendor and wealth. Also known as the Church of the Divine Wisdom, it was considered the center of the eastern Christian church.

Constantine's own mother during a trip to the Holy Land.

Over the centuries, the city continued to prosper and grow. Later emperors, such as Justinian the Great (A.D. 527–565) added to the city's incredible architecture. Justinian's reconstruction of the Hagia Sophia stood as his crowning achievement. The largest church of its day, the Hagia Sophia rose 180 feet (55 meters) to the peak of its massive dome. It took 10,000 workmen a span of six years to complete it. Elaborately decorated with golden lampstands and other religious artifacts, the Hagia Sophia was the centerpiece of Christianity in Constantinople.

All this construction could be possible only in a city

as wealthy as Constantinople, which was a great trading capital. The trade routes of Byzantium connected the city and its productive populace with the traders and merchants of Europe, Asia, and Africa. Its Roman roads carried imports of goods from places as far as Iceland to the northwest, Ethiopia in Africa to the south, and China to the east. All major trade caravans—those from China, Persia, and India—passed through the gates of the majestic city. Sea routes also connected Constantinople with traders, including the spice merchants of India and the Far East. African gold, Spanish olive oil, Frankish wine, Egyptian cotton, Russian furs, German grain, and jewels from China were all found in the marketplace of Constantinople. Hundreds of shops lined its main street, where luxury items of all kinds were sold. The city's docks and wharves were home to sailors and merchants from every corner of the ancient world.

This trade helped win Constantinople a place as one of the richest empires in the world. Not only did the Byzantines have great wealth in the form of trade goods, but they also produced a gold coin noted for its constant value. Called the *bezant* (after the word *Byzantine*), the coin contained 65 grains of pure gold. Introduced by Constantine the Great, it became an accepted form of currency all over the trading world. For nearly 700 years, the bezant provided monetary security for the sprawling trade empire of Byzantium.

To its neighbors, Constantinople stood as a symbol of prosperity, security, Christian faith, and power. Even though the city and the larger Byzantine Empire played an important role in the trade, religion, and political power of the East, it was also the object of envy, jealousy, and even bitter hatred from its rivals. For that reason, Constantinople used an extensive system of fortifications, soldiers, ships, and sailors to protect the empire. Every man in Byzantium under the age of 40 was required to serve in the military. Throughout much of Byzantine history, the military regularly employed mercenaries as well. Such paid recruits might come from as far away as England or the eastern reaches of Russia.

At its peak of strength, the Byzantine army was 120,000 strong, with its soldiers divided into regiments of 3,000 to 4,000 men. Troops were equipped with a variety of weapons, including bows and arrows, broadswords and shields, daggers, javelins, maces, and slings. The army relied heavily on its cavalry. The horsebound riders carried lances, bows, swords, and battle-axes. These cavalry troops were highly skilled at shooting their bow and arrows even as their horses galloped at top speed.

As an incentive to continue their service, the empire gave plots of land to soldiers who took posts in the far corners of the empire. On this land, they could establish their own farms and villas, complete with slaves and servants. They could also collect taxes from the peasants who worked their lands. Such landholdings were held for life and could be passed on to an heir, as long as he was willing to serve in the army as his father had.

The Byzantines were highly trained combatants. As early as the sixth century A.D., the Byzantine military published its first handbook for soldiers. The manual warned officers, including generals, to pursue the enemy with caution and to avoid full-scale battle whenever possible. They were encouraged to spare the lives of prisoners and to treat female captives with respect. Generals were also told to use propaganda to keep up their troops' spirits. They were encouraged to make up stories about other regiments and allies who had won fictitious battles.

Those Byzantine soldiers who engaged the enemy in battle carried special banners to rally the patriotic feelings of the army. The Roman standard, known as the *vexillum*, was considered essential for good luck in a battle. Regimental chaplains and priests were present to help the troops pray and sing patriot songs. The Christian infantry, as it advanced across a field toward an enemy army, often chanted: "The Cross shall conquer!"

Although the Byzantine army and navy were generally used to defend the borders of the empire from outside

The Byzantine Empire's Secret Weapon

No weapon or tactic used by the Byzantine military was more feared than the mysterious liquid known as Greek Fire. Created through a secret formula by a Greek Syrian named Callinicus of Heliopolis, Greek Fire became a standard weapon for the Byzantine army and navy. No one today knows exactly what elements were included in this highly explosive and flammable liquid. It may have included naphtha, sulfur, saltpeter (later used to make gunpowder), quicklime, and various oil products. Greek Fire was used in battle in a variety of ways. It could be poured into clay pots and launched by catapult toward an enemy position, where it would explode and spread searing flames as the pots broke on impact. The fire it created could not be extinguished with water; in fact, water caused the fires to burn with greater intensity. The incendiary device could also be thrown by hand and squirted out of tubes.

Because of its unstable nature, Greek Fire would sometimes burst into flames accidentally, killing Byzantine forces as well as their enemies. In time, the army dropped Greek Fire as a weapon because it was considered too dangerous to transport on land. The navy, on the other hand, used it effectively for hundreds of years. In just one year alone, A.D. 941, the Byzantines used Greek Fire to destroy 10,000 Russian ships. Frightened Russian sailors called the explosive weapon "lightning from heaven." The eleventh-century Byzantine Emperor Alexius I Comnenus used the fiery substance in a naval battle against Italian ships from Pisa. Alexius mounted bronze lion heads on the bows of his ships and had Greek Fire sprayed through tubes attached to the lions' open mouths, making it look to the Pisans like the gleaming lion heads were belching fire.

This mosaic, which graces the walls of Constantinople's Hagia Sophia, depicts Emperors Constantine and Justinian the Great at the side of the Virgin Mary and the infant Jesus Christ. The church's artwork celebrated the city's place as a center of the Christian world, and also remembered the deeds of past leaders.

invasion, emperors sometimes used their military strength to try to gain more territory as well. One emperor who did this was Justinian I, who reigned from 527 to 565. During the sixth century, Justinian launched a series of brilliant military campaigns to regain portions of the western Roman Empire. His generals won significant victories against the Germanic Vandals and Ostrogoths, as well as the Berbers of North Africa. Justinian's forces also took possession of the Mediterranean islands of Corsica, Sardinia, and the Balearics. Even the southern portion of Spain fell under Byzantine rule.

Despite such military and political successes, the Byzantine Empire was still a frequent target of invasion from many different forces. For 500 years after the reign of

Justinian, Byzantium fought to retain control of its territory.

Of all the enemies of Constantinople, none came to be feared more than the armies of Islam. These soldiers, most of whom were mounted tribal warriors from central Arabia, practiced the religion founded by the great Arab prophet of the seventh century, Muhammad. The religion was called Islam. Just a decade following Muhammad's death in 632, Islamic warriors, or Muslims, ravaged the Byzantine-controlled states of Egypt, Persia, Palestine, and Syria. As they did so, the Arabs stripped land away from the Byzantine Empire forever. The city of Constantinople itself was besieged by Islamic armies in a series of assaults between 673 and 677, but the decisive actions of the Byzantine navy and their use of Greek Fire were able to keep the city from falling. Even so, the Muslims were successful in other campaigns. In fact, Muslim forces fought so fiercely against their Byzantine foes that, by A.D. 711, the Byzantine Empire had shrunk to include only Anatolia (largely modern-day Turkey), Greece, and the Balkan States to the west of the Aegean Sea.

It was in 717 that the Muslims returned in force, again laying siege to Constantinople. This time, the city was saved by a general from Anatolia (the peninsula of Asia Minor) who led his men against the Muslims, pushing them nearly off the Anatolian peninsula. In 717, he was crowned as the new emperor of Byzantium, Leo III (who reigned 717–741).

Despite Leo's victories against the Muslims, including the help he gave to the city of Constantinople, the Islamic campaigns caused extraordinary changes in Byzantium. By the end of the eighth century, Byzantium had been reduced to a rather small state, and it had little power to wage offensive war. It had also lost much of its claim as the inheritor of Roman power. On Christmas Day, 800, a Frankish leader known as Charlemagne was crowned by the Roman Catholic pope as the new Roman emperor. Few Byzantines thought of Charlemagne, the emperor in the West, as the rightful heir of the Roman Empire. However, there was little Constantinople could do, since it no longer controlled the lands of the former western empire of Rome or even the Middle East. Instead, Byzantium had shrunk to the status of a Greek empire.

The decline in the fortunes of Constantinople seemed to turn around in the ninth century, though. The next 200 years—from 867 to 1056—was a period of prosperity for Byzantium. More trade than ever before poured through the Byzantine-controlled straits, creating great wealth. Even military campaigns against the Muslims met with success. When the new Slavic state of Russia was created in the tenth century, its monarchy soon allied itself with Constantinople's emperors. A great Byzantine leader, Basil II (976–1025), ruled for nearly 50 years and fought to win additional territory for his empire. Fighting in both the east and west, Basil II conquered the Bulgarians and annexed Balkan territory. During his Bulgarian campaign, he took 14,000 prisoners, blinded them all, then sent them back to their king, who went mad that the sight of his vanquished and humiliated army. He also fought the Arabs in Syria, bringing further additions of territory to Byzantium.

Once again, Byzantium was a wealthy, secure, and splendid state. Despite such successes, though, the future of the Byzantine Empire remained uncertain.

An Empire
in Decline

Despite the fact that Constantinople was a major Christian city, it had split with the western Church in Rome over certain religious issues. The ill feelings between the two Christian centers helped encourage soldiers of the Fourth Crusade, which began in 1203, to attack Constantinople, rather than march directly to the Holy Land to confront the Muslims.

Old and new enemies rose to the front. By the mid-eleventh century, two great forces—the Muslims in the East, and the Normans, or Vikings, in the West—were menacing Constantinople. Although neither succeeded in bringing down the empire, the Normans gained control of Italy and the Muslim Turks came to dominate Anatolia. This loss to the Muslims was particularly troublesome to the Byzantines, since many of their soldiers came from the upland plains of Anatolia. The victory of the Normans came at a high price as well. The Italian city-state of Venice had aided the Byzantines in their campaign against the Normans, but only after being promised extensive trading rights within Byzantium. As a result, Byzantine trade was weakened.

19

During this same period, the links between the Western Church of Rome and Eastern Christianity centered in Constantinople were finally severed. The two Christian forces could not agree on key religious issues. When the pope made Charlemagne the emperor of Rome in 800, few people in the West gave any serious thought to Eastern Christianity. It was as if Eastern and Western Christianity were two completely different religions. This split led to problems for Constantinople during the Crusades. In 1096, the Catholic Church in the West called upon Christians to make a crusade to free the Holy Land of Palestine and Jerusalem from Muslim control. The First Crusade lasted until 1099, and others followed. The Fourth Crusade, which began in 1203, resulted in the pillaging of Constantinople by Christian Crusaders from the West.

When the Christian knights arrived in Italy on their way to the Holy Land and Egypt, they found that they were unable to pay the high costs the people of Venice charged for passage across the Mediterranean Sea. The Venetian leader (doge) Enrico Dandolo agreed to make a deal with the Crusaders, however. Dandolo had been blinded 30 years earlier by the Byzantines when he was held prisoner in Constantinople. His captors had aimed the rays of the sun through a concave mirror into Dandolo's eyes, destroying his vision. Dandolo convinced the Crusaders to attack the Christian city of Constantinople instead of Muslim strongholds in the Holy Land.

The Crusaders' assault on the city was merciless. Western European soldiers ransacked every type of building in Constantinople, from palaces to churches. They set many fires, ruining the art and architecture of the ancient city. When they returned to their homelands in Europe, they brought with them treasures of gold, silver, precious gems, and furs that they had stripped from Constantinople. For the next 50 years, the Byzantine Empire was ruled by

Western Europeans as a Latin kingdom. With the devastation of the once great and powerful city, the glory days of Byzantium were over.

As the Byzantine Greeks eventually tried to restore their lost power, the new Byzantium remained a shadow of its former self. Through the 1100s, Constantinople had been a dazzling city. After the Fourth Crusade, however, the city lost its wealth and political dominance. The 1300s saw civil wars and emperors dethroned. In 1347, the bubonic plague, known as the Black Death, struck at the heart of the Byzantine Empire, killing as many as two out of every three people. Once again, the Muslim Turks began to menace the weakened empire. Their armies drove deep into Byzantine territory to attack a nearly defenseless Constantinople. In fact, by this point, the empire consisted of little more than the city of Constantinople itself. Only a few other cities and towns, such as the wealthy Thessalonica, were still under Byzantine control.

The great culture of Byzantium was no more. Its political power had vanished; its once-striking architecture lay in ruins. The trade routes had been cut off and overrun. The imperial leaders of the city were reduced to a second-rate status. When a new emperor, John VI, and his wife were crowned in Constantinople in 1347, the jewels in their crowns were nothing more than glass fakes. In the West, the kings, bishops, even the pope, paid little attention to Constantinople. By 1400, the city was a place of gloom and despair whose people lacked a sense of hope for the future.

Seeing that the Byzantine Empire was greatly weakened, the Turkish Muslims were soon at the gates of Constantinople once again. They surrounded the city during the summer of 1402. Only the advance of a Mongolian army that had defeated the Ottoman Turks in battle at Ankara saved the beleaguered Byzantine city. Disputes and power struggles between various Turkish factions kept them from organizing another siege for a decade or so. Then, in 1413, a new sultan (Turkish ruler) came to power. By 1422, the people of Constantinople found that the Muslims had surrounded their city yet again. This siege ended almost as quickly as it had started, however. The sultan, Murad II, had to end the siege after a rebellion at home and some other palace intrigues took place. Murad packed up his soldiers and left the ancient city. Once again, outside circumstances and forces had bought the Byzantines additional time.

The advance of the Muslims against the Byzantines finally achieved some success in the 1420s, however. After

In the Shadow of Former Splendor

A walk through the ancient streets of Constantinople told visitors the story. Although the city had boasted a population of nearly one million residents in the 1100s, by 1400, its people numbered only about 100,000. Churches were crumbling. The royal palace was so run-down, it was considered unlivable. Many buildings no longer had roofs, because the lead had been sold to foreigners for quick cash in earlier years. The once-glorious chariot track, the Hippodrome, was just a dilapidated remnant where young noblemen went to play polo. There were still many shops and stores in the city, but they were often owned and run by foreigners, such as Venetians, who sent the profits out of the city.

There were bright spots, however. A few grand mansions and estates still stood. Some of the old monasteries and nunneries had been kept in good order and their residents continued to produce well-crafted books and other materials for learning. The rich could still be seen in the city's streets as they were carried about in fancy litters by servants, in the same way that their wealthy ancestors had traveled for hundreds of years. Thousands of Christian pilgrims still visited the city each year, eager to see the city's ancient churches and relics. The 1,000-year-old Church of the Divine Wisdom, the Hagia Sophia, also remained a sight to behold. Its beauty and artistic treasures had been faithfully maintained over the centuries.

Murad ended the siege of Constantinople, an opportunity arose in 1430 for the Muslims to capture the Byzantine city of Thessalonica, one of the last of the significant Byzantine urban centers. The city's governor, a physically weak hypochondriac named Andronicus, fearing he would lose his city to the Turks, instead sold it to the Italian city-state of Venice. The Venetians were unable to protect it either, and Thessalonica fell to the Turks. Constantinople could do little but watch its neighboring city topple, knowing that its own future was uncertain.

In 1448, Byzantine Emperor John VIII Palaeologus died. He had served as emperor through a trying generation for the empire. He had fought Turkish advances and had worked hard to bring the Roman Catholic Church of the West and its pope into a mutual religious alliance with his own Eastern Christian empire. His efforts had failed. At his death, events began to take place that would eventually bring about the final siege of Constantinople.

John VIII had been the oldest of six brothers when he became emperor. By the time he died, two of the brothers were dead; one of them had died just three months earlier. Of the three remaining brothers—Demetrius, Thomas, and Constantine—only Constantine was qualified to take the throne of Byzantium. Thomas had served only as a weak provincial ruler, and Demetrius had actually helped lead a Turkish campaign to besiege Constantinople in 1442.

At John VIII's death, Constantine came to power. He was already an old man for the time, in his mid-forties. Little is known of his physical appearance, but he seems to have been tall and lean, with a dark complexion and a face that bore strong family features. He had already proven himself to be a capable soldier and government administrator. Although he was never known as a deep thinker or philosopher, he was an honest man who had a reputation for integrity, patience, kindness, and generosity. Constantine became popular with his subjects, who willingly served him with affection and loyalty. Three months after John's death, Constantine was crowned as emperor in the Byzantine town of Mistra. In March 1449, Constantine entered the city that bore his name.

Within two years of the rise of Constantine (now Constantine XI) in 1451, a new Turkish sultan came to power. He was known as Sultan Mehmet II. At the time he began his reign, Mehmet was a youth of 19.

Born in Adrianople on March 30, 1432, Mehmet's father had been a powerful sultan and his mother had been a slave. Mehmet had an unhappy childhood. His father ignored him, favoring his other sons, whose mothers were of royal blood. When both of his half brothers died, Mehmet was in line to become sultan. Because his chances of inheriting the throne had always been remote, if not impossible, he had never been properly educated. Mehmet's father immediately ordered that he be tutored. Over the next several years, some of the best available teachers taught Mehmet philosophy, the sciences, Islamic and Greek literature, and government. He became fluent in five or six languages, including the eastern forms of Greek, Arabic, Persian, and Hebrew, as well as the language of the West, Latin.

Mehmet's father, Murad, had been a man of peace. He was more a philosopher than a national leader and had always tried to pursue a life of quiet reflection and meditation. In fact, on two occasions, once when Mehmet was 12 and again when he was 16, his father had abdicated the throne to his son in order to devote himself full-time to study and reflection. However, the young Mehmet was too immature to rule. As a teenager, he was arrogant, ruthlessly ambitious, and jealous of everyone around him. Mehmet proved himself so unfit for leadership that his chief advisor, Halil Pasha, a trusted friend of his father's, pleaded with Murad to return to his throne. The old sultan did so, and banished his unruly son from his court for two years.

When Sultan Mehmet II came to power in 1451, he was not even out of his teens. Despite his age, he was an ambitious ruler and set out to plan a siege of Constantinople almost immediately.

When his father died of a stroke during a fitful rage on February 13, 1451, Mehmet became the new sultan. He was crowned in Adrianople during a grand reception in the sultan's palace. Once there, he installed advisors who would serve him loyally. Among them was Halil Pasha. Although no one intended to challenge Mehmet for the throne, he insured his power by having his father's most recent wife's four-year-old son smothered in the bath.

At age 19, Mehmet was a handsome youth of average height but with a powerful figure. His face was marked by a narrow hooked nose, curving eyebrows, and full lips. His appearance was described as similar to a parrot eating ripe,

red cherries, with fiery eyes. He could be extremely digni-
fied in a public setting, but he already had a reputation as a
heavy drinker. Mehmet also became known for enjoying
the company of philosophers and artists.

At the same time, Mehmet was a paranoid man, almost
irrational in his desire for privacy and secrecy. He pursued
his goals without any thought of whether they would be
popular within his sultanate. Mehmet never allowed any-
thing to stand in his way. Once he put his mind to a task,
there was no stopping him. Soon, he would set out to
accomplish the greatest task of his reign: to force the fall of
the ancient Christian city of Constantinople.

The young sultan's father, Murad, had always been on
good terms with Constantinople. Before Mehmet had been
in power even one year, however, he had begun to plot
the siege and fall of Constantinople. Using the powers of
diplomacy he had been taught in his rigorous education,
Mehmet worked hard to make treaties with several Western
powers in an effort to isolate Constantinople from the rest of
Europe. He was successful in signing treaties with the
Hungarians and the Venetians. From those victories, he set
out to limit Constantinople's options for the future. By early
winter of 1451, Mehmet ordered the erection of a fortress
complex along the banks of the Bosporus, the 18-mile-long
(29-kilometer-long) narrow strait connecting the Sea of
Marmara with the Black Sea. Its location was strategic.
Constantinople had controlled the seagoing traffic into and
out of the Black Sea for hundreds of years. With the kind
of fortification Mehmet was building, the Turkish sultan
could gain the power to dominate the trade himself. To
construct such a fort would also be a first step in his long-
range plans to lay siege to the city and finally destroy the
Byzantine Empire.

The fortress was built at the narrowest part of the
Bosporus, a place then referred to as Boghaz-kesen, or the

Cutter of the Throat. Construction began in the spring of 1452. To make way for the new complex, the sultan ordered the destruction of Byzantine churches and monasteries. Workmen used the masonry rubble from the Byzantine structures to build the foundations of the fortress castle.

As the people of Constantinople heard about the castle the sultan's men were erecting, they became anxious, even fearful, that another Turkish siege would soon follow. There was little that Emperor Constantine could do to prevent it, though. He sent ambassadors to meet with the sultan, but he refused to meet with them. Constantine took a bold step and ordered that all Turkish people living in Constantinople be put in prison. He later released them, realizing that such a move meant nothing to Mehmet. Desperate for some sign of good will from the sultan, Constantine sent representatives with gifts to make a plea to Mehmet that the Greek villages near the sultan's new fortress complex be left alone. Again, the sultan made no promises. By summer, Constantine had decided to send another delegation to ask Mehmet to assure the Byzantines that the castle being built was not a signal that the sultan was soon to lay siege to Constantinople. To make his intentions perfectly clear to the Byzantine emperor, Mehmet had Constantine's ambassadors executed by decapitation. Constantine sent no more envoys to the sultan.

By the end of August 1452, the sultan's fortress was completed. Mehmet immediately began to threaten Constantinople. He boldly marched his army from his fortress to the very gates of the Byzantine city. There, he set up camp with his men for three days. As the Byzantines watched worriedly from their positions on the ancient city walls, the sultan's engineers examined the walls and defenses that protected the city. Both those inside and outside the city understood very well what lay ahead.

The Sultan
Sets the Stage

ⲟⲩⲁ
ⲓⲫⲓⲛⲉⲩⲟⲛⲓⲁⲥ·-
ⲃⲓⲱⲧⲟⲟⲣ·

Long before the fifteenth-century siege of Constantinople, the Arabs had fought the Byzantines. This illustration of a Greek naval battle comes from a Greek manuscript from the eleventh century.

That same fall of 1452, the sultan placed three large cannons on the walls of his own fortress on the banks of the Bosporus and announced that all ships would have to pay him to pass through the straits. The castle had made him the new master of the region and its trade. In November, when a Venetian ship attempted to go through the strait without paying the sultan, the cannons opened fire, sank the ship, and took the crew prisoner. All the sailors were decapitated except for the captain, who was impaled on a stake beside the Bosporus, in sight of all passing ships. Like Constantinople, Venice seemed helpless to fight back against the sultan's bullying. In fact, none of the Italian city-states seemed ready, willing, or even able to come to the aid of the Byzantines to present a united force against the Turks and to stop the sultan's plans to conquer Constantinople.

Even with the successful construction of his fortress along the Bosporus, the sultan knew that a siege of Constantinople would not be an easy task. Others had attempted such sieges and failed. Mehmet understood how expensive a lengthy siege could be. He also knew that, if he failed, the honor of his Ottoman Empire would be lost. He pondered the question of whether to attempt a siege over a period of several weeks during the winter of 1452–1453. By the end of January, he called his old teacher, the vizier (high executive official) Halil, and announced: "Only one thing I want. Give me Constantinople." For the 21-year-old sultan of the Ottoman Turks, the ancient city of the Byzantines had become an obsession.

Preparations began for the fateful siege of Constantinople. Both the Byzantines inside and the Turks outside organized their plans with haste. The sultan began to assemble a great navy near Gallipoli (a peninsula in Turkey between the Dardanelles and Saros Gulf). Old, creaky ships were refitted, and new vessels—huge triremes—joined the fleet. Triremes were large warships, originally designed by the ancient Greeks. They featured three rows of oarsmen who propelled the ships swiftly through the water, then rammed enemy vessels. Mehmet's navy also included biremes, galleys, and fustae, or long boats, known to be fast and easy to maneuver. Just how many ships the sultan gathered at Gallipoli is disputed. The best accounts say the fleet had more than 120 vessels. Some of the rowers in the Turkish navy were slaves or prisoners of war, but many of them had volunteered to take part in Mehmet's campaign.

While the fleet came together at Gallipoli, an enormous Turkish army also assembled. Few armies of the day could have matched the sultan's. Estimates vary, but the Turks may have numbered as many as 120,000, of which about

In preparation for the siege of Constantinople, Mehmet built new ships for his navy, including powerful triremes like this one. Named for their three tiers of oars, triremes were first built in Corinth. The ancient warships were often used by Greeks and Romans.

80,000 were seasoned troops. Even the biggest, best-trained army was only as efficient as its weapons. The sultan had ordered blacksmiths and armorers to make all the necessary instruments of war during the winter months before the siege. They produced thousands of swords, shields, helmets, breastplates, spears, and javelins. Military engineers kept busy building machines for the coming war. These included battering rams and ballistas—huge launchers, similar to large crossbows, designed to shoot long missiles of iron.

Despite these painstaking preparations, a large navy and a well-armed army would not necessarily ensure Mehmet success in his planned siege. Perhaps the single most important factor in the coming siege would be cannons. Cannons were not new to European warfare in 1453. Some models had come into use in combat over a century earlier. Early cannons were too small to effectively destroy masonry walls. Thus, the first cannons in Europe were used to scatter and kill troops on the battlefield, to damage enemy vessels (rarely were they able to sink them), and to kill or wound navy crewmen. As he began early in his reign to plan for the siege of Constantinople, Mehmet realized that larger cannons were crucial.

The man Mehmet hired to build the huge siege cannon for the Turks was a Hungarian named Urban. A trained engineer, Urban had offered his services first to the emperor of Byzantium, but when Constantine was unable to raise the money to pay Urban, the military engineer made the Turks a similar offer. Mehmet saw Urban's skill and employed him, paying him four times as much as Urban had asked from Constantine. In just a few months, Urban had built the cannon that was used at the newly constructed Turkish fortress on the Bosporus to sink the Venetian ship that had attempted to run the Muslim blockade.

Despite the new cannon's power, Mehmet wanted an even larger one for his siege. Urban set to work building a cannon twice as large as his earlier models. It was ready by January 1453, and it was immense. Its barrel was over 26 feet (8 meters) in length, with 8 inches (20 centimeters) of bronze wrapped around the barrel to keep the weapon from blasting apart when fired. The barrel's circumference measured over 30 inches (76 centimeters) at its base and nearly 100 inches (254 centimeters) at its mouth, where the cannonball was inserted. The cannonballs were made from granite and were said to have weighed 1,200 pounds (544 kilograms). Once it was built, Mehmet had the cannon transported to his palace. The muscle of 700 men was needed just to load the cannon on a cart. Its sheer weight required 15 pairs of oxen to pull it on the cart.

Once the cannon arrived at the sultan's residence, he was eager to see a demonstration of its explosive power. The cannon was loaded—a process that required 134 pounds (61 kilograms) of gunpowder and hours of difficult work. The people living near Adrianople were warned to expect a loud noise from the cannon's blast and to not be frightened by it. When it was fired, the exploding cannon could be heard more than 10 miles (16 kilometers) away. It lobbed a ball an entire mile (1.6 kilometers), and when the cannonball smacked into the earth, it left a crater 6 feet (1.8 meters) deep. Mehmet was highly pleased. He ordered hundreds of workers to begin to level the road between Adrianople and Constantinople to help ease the transport of the great siege cannon. To smooth the way for the cannon, bridges had to be reinforced to support its weight. Two hundred men accompanied the weapon to protect it and keep it from slipping as 60 oxen pulled it on the cart. By March 1453, the cannon had arrived near Constantinople, along with smaller cannons that had been built in Turkish foundries under Urban's direction.

With the artillery delivered, the sultan's army also began to arrive. Mehmet himself set out for the Byzantine capital on March 23. He reached the outskirts of the city on April 5. He was very excited about the coming campaign, and the men were in high spirits. Everything was in place and ready to blast away at the ancient, crumbling walls of the capital of Byzantium. The siege of Constantinople was at hand.

Throughout the months that the Turks planned, organized, and put into effect the elements of their planned siege, the people inside the city walls of Constantinople had been busy, too. During the winter of 1452–1453, the Byzantines improved their defenses by cleaning out their old moats and reinforcing the crumbling city walls. Weapons were given out to those most capable of fighting.

Special funds were collected by the city government, as well as by churches and monasteries, to pay for the cost of the city's defense. Determined to do something to help, Emperor Constantine tried to drum up support for the city from the Italian city-states and other Christian centers of the West. Little help arrived. Pope Nicholas was unable to send military aid and was in no hurry to help members of the Eastern Orthodox Church. That arm of the Christian world had been at odds with the Western Catholics for hundreds of years. By the time the council of the city-state of Venice decided to send several ships of supplies to aid Constantinople, it was too late: The siege had already been in progress for two weeks. The desperately needed ships never reached the city.

Some support from the West did come to help rescue Constantinople. A Catholic cardinal recruited and sent 200 troops to the city's aid. Other foreign soldiers, some of them mercenaries for hire, also arrived to help defend the ancient city. A Spanish nobleman named Don Francisco de Toledo came with some others to fight, too. Against a force of more than 100,000 well-armed Turks, however, these reinforcements were, in the end, insignificant.

If Constantinople had few outside allies willing to help, the situation inside the city was almost as disheartening. Not even all those who actually lived in Constantinople stayed to fight. In late February, seven ships loaded with 700 Italian knights and sailors abandoned the city. On the eve of the siege, Constantinople had 26 warships anchored in the waters of the Golden Horn, accompanied by a scattering of smaller vessels and trade ships. Only ten of them were actually Byzantine.

When the emperor ordered a count of all the city's fighting men, his secretary, Phrantzes, discovered a shocking fact: Only 5,000 Greeks were available for combat, plus another 2,000 foreign troops. Among these men were monks, some of whom were forcibly armed against their wills. When he received the report, a stunned Constantine told Phrantzes not to let the people know the number of troops, lest for fear that the public would panic. Nearly everyone in the city already knew the harsh truth facing the Byzantines, however: 7,000 men would now have to defend 14 miles of city walls against an army of more than 100,000 Muslims who were armed with some of the largest siege cannons on the face of the earth.

April 1, 1453, was Easter Sunday. The people of the city celebrated the holiday with a cautious eye toward the Turkish camps. It had been a pleasant spring, and the city's orchards were fragrant with blossoms. In the distance, though, the Turkish army turned toward Constantinople. The next day, the advance forces began to arrive within

A Great Warrior From Genoa

Though Western European governments were less than enthusiastic about helping the Byzantines, some brave individuals did come to the city's aid. A well-known soldier from Genoa, Giovanni Longo Giustiniani, delivered two Genoese ships filled with 700 well-trained fighting men to Constantinople by late January 1453. Giustiniani was a young member of one of the most powerful families of Genoa. He was known for his skill in defending walled cities, so the emperor immediately made him commander over the defense of all of Constantinople's land walls. During the siege, Giustiniani took up position at the Mesoteichion portion of the wall, where the action would prove intense. More than once, he rallied his men in defense of Muslim assaults. This brave Genoan became one of the most heroic defenders of the city. His presence on the walls of the city was so important that, during the final assault of the Turks, when the Genoan commander was severely wounded by a bullet fired from a Turkish culverin (a type of musket), a general panic spread among the defenders, which allowed the ultimate collapse of the city.

sight of the Byzantine troops manning the ramparts along the city's walls. A small skirmish outside the city drew the first blood of the siege, and the outnumbered defenders fled inside the city gates for shelter. Constantine ordered the moat bridges to be burned and the gates locked. The siege was drawing near.

Even though Sultan Mehmet could take comfort in knowing that he vastly outnumbered the Byzantines in terms of troops and ships, he also understood that the defenses of Constantinople were formidable. The city sat on a wedge of land that jutted out to the east, facing the Sea of Marmara, creating a triangle bounded by water on two sides. Most of the city's major buildings were clustered on the easternmost corner of the jutting triangle. Fourteen miles of well-designed and fortified walls, bristling with 50 protected gates, encircled the city. Most of the walls were old, dating back to the fifth century. They had been erected to protect Constantinople from invading tribes of Germans, such as the Goths. For a millennium, the walls had protected the city. Where the city flanked the sea, a single wall bordered Constantinople. Here, the city's navy provided the first line of defense. On the remaining side, which faced land to the west, the Byzantines had erected a wall that was far more complex. If enemy forces attacked from that side, they would first face a moat measuring 60 feet (18 meters) across and 22 feet (7 meters) deep. This moat normally remained empty, but could be hurriedly filled with water pipes. Archers manned a low wall that ran along the city-side of the moat. Thirty feet behind them stood a second wall that towered nearly 27 feet (8 meters) high. The second wall was defended by additional troops, who could also fire arrows through a series of arched openings that flanked a line of towers spaced 50 and 100 feet (15 to 31 meters) apart. Twenty feet (6 meters) behind the second wall stood a massive third wall that rose 70 feet

This is a view of the ancient walls that had been built to defend the city of Constantinople. Although the walls had long been a strong defense against invading forces, by the time the Turks besieged the city in 1453, the development of new kinds of weapons reduced the walls' effectiveness.

(21 meters) high, and had even larger, stronger masonry towers. Although any attacker would have to face the moat and three great walls of increasing height, the walls were built eight centuries before gunpowder had begun to be used in European combat. Now the Turks were armed with siege cannons capable of blasting the old walls to rubble.

During earlier sieges, enemy attacks against the walls had failed. As a result, the emperor and his military advisors assumed the land walls would be able to fend off the brunt of the Turkish offensive. They placed many of the city's defenders along the ramparts of the land wall system. The emperor took a position on the northern end of the land wall at the Mesoteichion section near where the Lycus River flowed into the city. As luck would have it, the sultan placed his encampment directly opposite this portion of the land wall, as well. He had his red and gold tent erected about a quarter of a mile distance from the wall. It was there that the Muslims placed several cannons, including their largest artillery piece. The Turks also dug a protective trench parallel to the land wall and built a short wall of wood to protect their positions from enemy fire.

The seawalls were sparsely manned by the Byzantines. There, the monks were assigned to places where attack seemed least likely. Several hundred Venetian and Genoese soldiers and sailors manned the seawalls flanking the Golden Horn. A Catholic cardinal named Isidore positioned himself with 200 soldiers at the eastern-most part of the city, known as Acropolis Point. This was a land formation flanked by the Golden Horn on the left and the Sea of Marmara on the right. It faced the Turkish fleet at the mouth of the Bosporus.

The city defenders were well-armed and they wore better armor than the Turks did. They had several catapults that they could use, as well as long cannons. There were several cannons in the city, but their use would be limited, since gunpowder was in short supply. The city defenders also discovered that when they fired their cannons, the recoil damaged the city's ancient walls.

Anchored along the banks of the Bosporus, the Turkish fleet stood ready. Its orders were to make certain that no enemy ships or supplies reached Constantinople. The Turks' work was simple since they outnumbered the enemy considerably. Within the first week of the siege, the number of vessels in the fleet grew as 200 additional ships sailed into the Bosporus, giving further aid to the Turks.

Early on the morning of April 6, the soldiers manning

the city's land walls watched as the Turkish army took up its positions. The Muslim's heavy guns were aimed at the city walls. Mehmet sent a courier to the emperor under a flag of truce. Mehmet promised that, if Constantine surrendered the city, he would spare the lives of the civilians. Should the emperor decide to ignore the sultan's offer, then Mehmet would make no assurances as to the safety of anyone inside Constantinople once it fell. Naturally, the Byzantine emperor refused to consider surrendering. Once his response was delivered to the sultan, the Muslims opened fire on the city. The siege of Constantinople had begun.

The Janissaries were an elite fighting force whose soldiers were fiercely loyal to the sultan. Janissaries were often recruited from the ranks of prisoners of war or Christian youths removed from their families and raised as Muslims. This engraving depicts the elaborate uniform of a Janissary commander.

The Battle Unfolds

The Turkish guns did severe damage to Constantinople's land walls as they concentrated their firepower on the Charisian Gate, located on the sultan's left flank. By the end of the second day of bombardment, the gate was nearly in ruins. Even so, once night fell, the sultan and his men could hear the sounds of the people of the city working to repair the day's damage. The Turks busied themselves with engineering work, as well. The sultan ordered his troops to fill the moat that ran below the city's outer wall with earth while other workers tunneled toward the wall, intending to weaken it and cause parts to collapse. The work of filling in the moat, or foss, was difficult for the Muslim workers, who were under constant assault. From the city walls, defenders launched stones, arrows, even Greek Fire (an inextinguishable stream of fire composed of chemicals) at their enemy. In addition, the knights along the walls were armed with small guns that fired between five and ten walnut-sized lead balls at the Muslim workers.

Outside the land walls, Byzantine troops had taken up positions in several small castles. These structures were assaulted early in the siege. The castle at Therapia, situated on a Bosporus hill, was soon overrun. Its 40 defenders were killed, their bodies impaled on stakes. Another castle, Studius, was also destroyed after only a few hours of fighting. There, 36 combatants were also impaled.

More Turkish cannons arrived as the siege proceeded. By April 12, the Turks had set up 14 cannon batteries, each of which held four guns. On that same day, the portion of the wall that was manned by the emperor himself was in shambles and the moat in front of it nearly filled. The soldiers, with help from civilians of the city, tried to build a wooden palisade to protect the gaps in the wall. They used building beams, barrel staves, and the Byzantine equivalent of sandbags: sacks filled with dirt.

For the Byzantine forces, one of the few bright spots in the early days of the siege was the success of their navy. In the Bosporus, the Turkish ships were unable to dominate the Byzantine vessels. The enemy's cannons could not inflict adequate damage on the larger Greek ships the Byzantines used. Since their ships were taller than the Turkish vessels, the Christian forces were also able to fire arrows and throw spears down on the Turks, inflicting heavy damage. When the Turks lobbed flaming brands (pieces of burning wood) onto the decks of the Byzantine vessels, well-organized bucket brigades put out the fires in short order. Finally, facing defeat, the Turkish commander ordered his ships to sail back into the Bosporus out of harm's way. Later, only after the Turks changed the angles at which

An Endless Barrage

For nearly six straight weeks, the sound of cannon bombardment was daily, relentless, and deafening. For the Turks, it was such a labor-intensive chore to load the guns that several hours usually passed between the shots fired from one cannon. Historian Ralph Vickers described the difficulties of using the artillery of that period:

Artillery was still primitive, and a cannon was an unpredictable monster. After each ear-shattering boom and belch of acrid black smoke, a gun would recoil violently on its platform of planks, often lurching into the mud. Immediately oil was poured down its barrel to cool the scorched metal lest it split. Then with much straining and grunting the cannon was realigned on its target. When the barrel cooled the muck was swabbed out. Then began the process of priming with powder—an exasperating task in a gusty downpour of rain—and loading the shot.

The great cannon built by Urban could only be fired about seven times a day, and each shot created a thick black cloud of billowing smoke. It was worth the effort. Every time a half-ton (508-kilogram) granite cannonball struck the outer face of a Byzantine wall, it did considerable damage. The stone balls broke into hundreds of pieces on contact, tearing down portions of the wall. The wall's defenders attempted to blunt the cannonballs' damage by hanging pieces of leather and woolen bales off the wall's sides. Nothing did much to minimize the destruction, however, especially since the Turks fired more cannonballs faster than the people in the city could make repairs. Ironically, once, when the great cannon was fired, an accidental explosion occurred, killing Urban, the cannon's designer.

their cannons fired were they able to sink some of the Byzantine ships.

As he had greater success on land than on water, the sultan began to prepare for a land assault against the wall. Nearly two weeks into the siege, on April 18, Mehmet ordered a night assault against the Byzantine positions near the Fifth Military Gate, along the banks of the Lycus. The scene was a dramatic one. Under a shroud of darkness, the Turks launched flares, lighting up the night sky and casting an eerie glow over the landscape. Muslim soldiers lined up in columns to the beat of drums and clanging cymbals.

The main assault group consisted of elite troops known as the Janissary Guard. The term *janissary* came from a Turkish word that meant "new forces." The Janissaries were the sultan's best soldiers. They were well equipped, highly trained, and fiercely loyal to the sultan. Created as a military unit a century earlier, the Janissaries served the sultan for life as professional soldiers. Recruited or kidnapped from Christian families living in the sultan's lands, young boys were raised as Muslims in private training schools, where they learned the arts of war. After they were separated from their parents, they lived in private barracks. Janissaries were forbidden to marry. Most would serve for years as part of the sultan's regiment of special guards.

Amid a shower of enemy spears, javelins, and stones thrown by catapults, the Janissaries rushed toward the city, shouting their battle cry. They carried torches to set fire to the wooden palisade in front of them. Some Janissaries had attached hooks to their spears to tear down the wooden barrier. Others carried ladders that they intended to take over the makeshift barricade. The battle along the wall was bloody. Despite their superior

SPAHIS

JANISSAIRES

The *spahis* (pronounced spuh-He) were Ottoman cavalry. The Janissaries were the sultan's best-equipped and best-trained troops, yet in spite of this they were unable to maneuver well in the narrow valley where the assault took place, and they were forced to withdraw.

numbers, the Turks were unable to maneuver well in the narrow valley where the assault took place. They soon found themselves bottled up. Unlike the Byzantines' uniforms, the Turks' uniforms included little armor. After four hours of brutal hand-to-hand combat, the Janissaries withdrew, defeated. They left behind 200 of their comrades, who were dead or wounded. Not one defender of Constantinople was killed in this first Turkish assault. For the time being, the possibility of victory over the Turkish forces looked promising for the defenders of the Byzantine capital.

The Janissaries' failure was a hard blow for the Turks. Even as they were being defeated, though, the forces of the sultan had fought bravely. What motivated these Muslim warriors to sacrifice themselves in such significant numbers? One answer lies in their religion. The Islamic faith of the fifteenth century taught the belief that a Muslim warrior's greatest act was to fight those who did not follow the teachings of Islam and did not recognize Muhammad as a great prophet. All Christians automatically fell into this category. The Muslims believed that, if they fought anyone considered an infidel, their sins would be forgiven. The greatest glory awaited those Muslim warriors who died fighting in the name of Allah (God) and Muhammad. These fallen combatants would go straight to heaven. In this otherworld paradise (*paradise* is, in fact, an Arab word), the warrior would be attended by dancing girls and other women who would take care of his every desire. The promise of such a reward motivated many Muslim warriors.

Two days after the Janissaries' defeat, the Muslims faced another loss, this one at sea. On April 20, soldiers on the seawalls spied four Christian ships on the distant horizon. Three of the vessels were Genoese galleys, sent by the pope and filled with much-needed supplies and weapons. The fourth was a great imperial transport, full of Sicilian grain. The ships stirred up excitement among the men along the walls. Turkish watchers also spotted the vessels, however. The sultan ordered a Bulgarian admiral named Baltoghlu to stop the Christian ships. Mehmet warned that if Baltoghlu failed in his mission and the four vessels reached the seawalls of Constantinople, he would be executed.

Throughout most of the day, a great sea battle took place. Although the Turks sent out dozens of ships, the larger Christian vessels were able to rain stones, javelins, and arrows upon their enemies. After the first hour of fighting, as the Genoese and Byzantine ships neared the city, the wind suddenly died off. The sails of the Christian vessels were left limp and useless. The Turkish ships, most of them propelled by hundreds of oarsmen, moved in for the kill. Seventy-five Turkish ships surrounded the three Genoese vessels. At one point in the raging battle, a trireme rammed the imperial transport, the largest and best armed of the four Christian ships. The sailors on the imperial transport made use of Greek Fire to fight back. They delivered the fiery substance with deadly force, causing enemy ships to burst into flames.

From shore, both the Byzantines and the Turks watched the battle unfold. Turkish sailors flung grappling hooks at the Christian ships, pulling enemy vessels into close contact. The four Christian vessels, repeatedly assaulted by dozens of Turks, still held fast. Ropes were tossed from one vessel to the other until the four were tied together, forming a seagoing castle, with each ship serving as a great tower. The assault against

The four Christian vessels sailed beyond their Muslim opponents toward the protective waters of the Golden Horn. Christians on shore cheered as the crippled ships entered the sanctuary of the strait.

them seemed to be endless, however. The sultan ordered fresh Turkish ships into the fray. Then, as evening broke at the end of an exhausting day of combat, the winds picked up again, refilling the sails of the four Christian vessels and turning the tide of battle.

Pushed by these new breezes, the four ships sailed beyond their Muslim opponents toward the protective waters of the Golden Horn. The Christians on shore cheered as the crippled ships entered the sanctuary of the strait. The day ended with another victory for the people of Constantinople.

The Turks had lost several ships. They had also suffered 400 casualties, including the deaths of 100 sailors. The Christian crews had had 23 deaths. Of the remaining crewmen, nearly one out of every two was wounded. The emperor was elated. His troops and allies had won a significant sea victory against overwhelming odds. This brought fresh hope to the people of the city. In addition, the four ships delivered new supplies of arms, food, and soldiers. The following account described the sultan's response to the recent events:

Mehmet returned to his tent filled with rage. The . . . consecutive reverses he had suffered were not only dangerously demoralizing his army, they were also undermining his own position in respect to Vizier Halil Pasha and other government ministers who had opposed the siege from the beginning. That same night Mehmet received a letter from Sheik Ak Shemseddin, one of the chief religious authorities in the camp, informing him that the troops were beginning to blame their Sultan for his misjudgment and lack of authority. Rumors began to spread throughout the Turkish camp that the siege might be abandoned.

Desperate for someone to blame, Mehmet turned on Baltoghlu. He summoned the defeated admiral to his tent. When Baltoghlu arrived, he was nursing a wound to the eye that he had received after being struck with a stone launched by one of his own men. The frightened admiral was certain of his fate. Mehmet launched into a tirade, browbeating the admiral and calling him a coward and an incompetent traitor. When Mehmet ordered Baltoghlu's execution by beheading, only the testimony of the admiral's men saved him from certain death. The sultan instead ordered the admiral disrobed and held on the ground by four slaves. Then, Baltoghlu received 100 blows with a golden rod on his bare back. Baltoghlu was then stripped of his rank and his personal possessions. His wealth was given to the Sultan's Janissary troops. He was forced to spend the remainder of his days in poverty.

After more than two weeks of siege, the Muslims realized that they were facing serious setbacks at the hands of the Christian defenders of the city. The Christian crews were more skilled and their ships superior. Turkish cannons were efficient, even deadly, but they required a great deal of labor and time between firing rounds. To make the Muslims' job more difficult, the people of Constantinople worked constantly to repair each day's damage.

As the sultan brooded about these problems, he realized that there was at least one more serious concern. As long as the Christians controlled access to the Golden Horn, the Muslims would never be able to approach the city from the northeast. To keep the Turks out of the Golden Horn, the Byzantines had stretched a huge heavy chain across the entrance to the Horn. One end of the chain was attached to the northern end of Constantinople, near the Gate of St. Barbara. The other end was located on the opposite shore, at the only one of Constantinople's

14 districts that was outside the city's main wall perimeter, a place called Pera. Pera had a wall of its own and, by 1453, it served as a base for Genoese traders and merchants. Once Mehmet decided that he could not remove the chain from the mouth of the Golden Horn by force, he set out on another plan—and it was brilliant. Under the advice of an Italian then serving Mehmet, the sultan concluded that Turkish ships should be dragged overland from the Bosporus to the Golden Horn, which would allow them to bypass the chain altogether.

It was a daunting task, however. Hundreds of men and oxen would have to haul the ships over a hilly ridge that ran 200 feet (61 meters) above sea level. The work began during the last week of April. Thousands of workers were already busy building a road from the Bosporus to the Golden Horn. They built special rolling cradles for the ships. By April 21, the work was nearly done. To hide what he was doing from the Genoese inside Pera, the sultan ordered his cannoneers to fire continuously, creating a wall of smoke that covered the actions of the Turks on land.

The next day, a Sunday, 70 of the sultan's boats began their overland journey. Using elaborate pulley systems and the muscle power of oxen and men, the ships creaked across dry land. What a strange sight this must have been. Each boat was loaded with a full crew, including oarsmen who stroked their oars against the air to the beat of drums, flutes, and trumpets, just as if they were passing across water. Most of the boats were triremes and biremes, but there were also several smaller craft. By noon, the sailors on the Christian ships and the people manning the city walls understood what was happening. They watched with shock and despair as the Turkish vessels slid into the waters of the Golden Horn.

The Byzantines and their allies were unsure how to counter the sultan's grand move. Now, Turkish ships were capable of blasting away at both the Christian ships and at the northeastern section of city walls. At last, a foreign galley captain named Giacomo Coco proposed a night raid against the Turkish vessels. The goal of the secret attack would be to set fire to the Muslim crafts and eliminate them as a threat to the city. The assault was postponed until the Venetians were ready to participate, losing precious time for the Byzantines. The raid took place on the night of April 28, just two hours before sunrise. It failed. The dozen or so ships, with their hulls partially protected from Turkish cannons by bales of cotton and wool, were caught and fired upon by the waiting Turks. The Turks had been warned of the secret raid by a Genoese traitor living in Pera. Christian and Muslim ships were destroyed, and dozens of Byzantine and Italian sailors drowned. When 40 such sailors swam to the Turkish shores, they were captured and killed later that day in sight of the city walls. In retaliation, the Byzantines paraded 260 Turkish prisoners up on the walls, then lopped the head off each of them as the sultan and his men watched in the distance.

The transporting of Muslim ships into the Golden Horn was a significant move by Mehmet. Now his ships could prevent any future Christian vessels from rescuing the city or supplying its people. This move also placed the Turkish navy between Constantinople and the Genoese trading city of Pera. Pera tried to remain neutral during the siege, but the city was constantly in an uncomfortable position. After all, the chain that had blocked the entrance into the Golden Horn across the strait from Constantinople had been anchored at Pera. Despite the city's neutrality, Genoese spies reported to both sides and traded with both parties, profiting from Pera's location.

With half of the sultan's ships inside the Golden Horn, the waterway no longer divided Mehmet's forces on either side of its banks. To link his armies more strongly, Mehmet ordered his men to build a pontoon bridge across the Horn. The bridge rested on 100 wine barrels roped together in pairs. Wooden beams and planks made up the walkway for the bridge. It was wide enough to carry men, carts, even cannons. In no time, the Muslims brought up cannons that could batter away at Constantinople's seawalls.

A Beleaguered City

The siege of Constantinople is depicted in this sixteenth-century wall painting. As the siege began, Turkish soldiers moved their cannons into strategic locations. As the siege continued, the Muslim Turks dug tunnels to try to get nearer to the city's walls. The Byzantines responded by flooding, caving in, or smoking out the tunnels, killing the Turks inside them.

For a week after the transport of the Muslim ships into the Golden Horn, the siege followed a repeated pattern in which the Turks bombed the city by day, and the Christian defenders made hurried repairs at night. There was little direct fighting and almost no casualties.

For the people inside the city, the critical problem soon became the shortage of food. By early May, the lack of food was so severe that the emperor requested special contributions from churches and wealthy individuals in Constantinople. Some money was raised, and officials gave the food that was available to the people, based on need. Still, the people looked to the days ahead and knew the harsh truth: If additional supplies did not reach the city soon, the Christians of Byzantium would have nothing to fear from the Muslims. Instead, they would simply starve to death.

The siege was taking its toll. The people were constantly aware of the seriousness of their plight. It was during these days that the emperor probably made contact with the sultan, through Genoese couriers from Pera, to discuss terms. The sultan continued to demand the unconditional surrender of the city. Mehmet did offer to allow Constantine to live once he gave over the capital, and promised the emperor a quiet retirement. Constantine refused. He did not intend to leave his

A Secret Mission to Save the City

With Constantinople running out of food and in dire need of military support, Emperor Constantine ordered a desperate mission. He dispatched a Venetian brigantine to sail out from the city in search of help and food. To trick the Muslims, the ship flew a Turkish flag and disguised its 12-man crew as Arabs. The ship left the Golden Horn on May 3 under cover of darkness. After the boom was removed near midnight, giving the brig clear passage into the Sea of Marmara, the vessel slipped past the enemy. The hopes of Constantinople's weary defenders now rested with this single ship and its secret mission.

Nearly three weeks later, on May 23, a crushing blow rocked the city. It did not come in the form of a cannon bombardment or another direct frontal assault, however. Wall watchers spotted a Venetian ship approaching the city, with Turkish vessels in hot pursuit. After nightfall, the chain was opened, and the vessel entered the relative safety of the Golden Horn. The ship was the same brigantine that had secretly left on its rescue mission. The ship did not bring good news to the excited people of Constantinople. Its crew had to give the Byzantines and their Italian allies the bad news: There would be no rescue from the West. If Constantinople were to survive, it would have to do so on its own.

defenseless city to the will of the Turkish ruler. Even when his own advisors suggested that it might be best for the emperor to escape while it was still possible, Constantine would hear none of it. At this crucial time for Byzantium, the emperor was determined to remain in the city—even if that meant death.

The Muslims continued to bombard the city through the early days of May, but Urban's great siege cannon was out of commission. According to an eyewitness to the events, a warrior named Nestor-Iskander, who kept a diary during the siege, "Since the great cannon fused well, the godless one issued orders to redeploy it. He ordered all of the army to march once more on the city and to make war for all days." By May 6, the monster artillery piece was fully operational, and once more, it was pounding the city walls. The next day, in the stillness of the night, the Turks mounted an assault on the city. As always, they concentrated their troops along the Mesoteichion section where the Lycus River flowed. Hundreds of Turks armed with lances, hooks, and scaling ladders, advanced across a section of the moat that they had filled with rubble and stones. Again, Nestor-Iskander described the action:

> As evening had already set in, the Turks began to fire from many cannons . . . and continued doing so through-out the entire night. They did not allow the townspeople to wall up that place. In the morning the Turks struck again with the great cannon and much of the wall tumbled down . . . As a large space was cleared, immediately a multitude of men rose, jumped into that place, and trampled one another. Similarly, the Greeks from the city fought face to face and roared like marvelous savages. It was frightful to see both their boldness and their vigor.

For three hours, the clash of arms went on without a break, but the Muslims were unable to break through.

Then the sultan moved his forces and concentrated on another section of the Constantinople wall, at a place called Blachernae, where the land wall and the seawall paralleled the Gold Horn. On May 12, Muslim land forces attacked after midnight; once again, they were unable to break through the complicated wall system of the city. To weaken the Blachernae for another attack, Mehmet ordered his cannon batteries to move from the Valley of the Springs outside the city walls of Pera to the shore opposite the Golden Horn, in order to bombard the Blachernae. After dragging the cannons across the wine-barrel bridge, the Turkish gunners opened fire. When they failed to damage the wall very badly, the sultan had the cannons moved to reinforce the other artillery machines located in the Lycus Valley.

As the warm days of May slipped past, the sultan renewed efforts to dig tunnels into the city. A lack of experienced miners in the sultan's army had hampered earlier efforts. When a commander arrived with a group of Serbian silver miners, however, the tunneling operation went into full swing. Such efforts never amounted to much. The defenders of the city repeatedly discovered the tunnels, and either caved them in, smoked out the miners, or flooded the tunnels, killing those trapped underground. On May 23, the Byzantines captured a group of miners and tortured their officer to get him to tell where all the Turkish mines were located. He did, and all the enemy tunnels were soon destroyed.

Turkish engineers did not spend all their time tunneling. On May 18, they added a new device to the sultan's arsenal of engineering feats. That morning, the Christian knights awoke to find a giant siege tower standing outside the Mesoteichion walls. The Turks had built it overnight. The wooden tower was covered with camel and oxen hides to protect it from fire. Although built to be used as an assault tower, complete with scaling ladders, ropes, and hooks, its first purpose was to protect the Turkish workers who were attempting to fill in the moat. By the end of the day, the tower had served this end well: the Turks had nearly finished building an assault road across the moat. That night, though, Christians sneaked out of the wall, placed several kegs of gunpowder at the base of the tower, and blew it up. The men inside were killed, and the tower fell to the ground in flames. The wall defenders then scattered much of the work accomplished by the Turks that day. Other attempts to build towers were not as successful for the Muslims. Assault towers never played an important role during the rest of the siege.

It was May 19, and the city was still in Christian hands. Its defenders had withstood repeated Turkish advances for over six weeks. With each passing day, however, despite their failures, the Turks seemed to be moving into better and better positions. They nearly controlled the Golden Horn. They had moved their army across a pontoon bridge to the city's walls. They had also destroyed at least a portion of the walls that many had considered impregnable. None of these moves had brought the Turks an ultimate victory. Still, they knew that they had one weapon at their disposal that the people of Byzantium did not have: time. Already, time was running out for the weary defenders of the last Christian stronghold of the ancient Roman Empire. As time passed, the defenders of Constantinople were beginning to run out of food, gunpowder and shot, patience, and—for some—even hope.

This medieval map of Constantinople speaks of the many centuries of besiegement the city had suffered: the extensive wall surrounding the city continues along the shoreline, warding off a potential attack from the sea.

The following days within the walls of Constantinople were disheartening. The people, many of whom believed in signs that might foretell the future, witnessed a series of events that they saw as ominous. An eclipse darkened the sky on the night of May 24. A great thunderstorm drenched the city, and was followed by a pounding hailstorm. On May 25, a heavy fog shrouded the city. All of these natural phenomena made some people believe God had turned his back on the city. Even so, as Orthodox Christians, most of the people of Constantinople sought comfort in their religion in this terrible time. According to Nestor-Iskander, "And in the company of prelates and the entire assembly, they took the sacred icons. They travelled along the walls of the city for the entire day and begged God's grace." Despite their prayers, the last shreds of hope began to slip away from the defenders of the city.

The Christians were not the only ones who were frustrated and disheartened, though. In spite of their successes, by the last week of May, the Turks were tired and discouraged, too. Their cannons had failed, even after weeks of bombardment, to bring down the walls of the city. Frontal assaults had been driven back, and the chain across the mouth of the Golden Horn was still securely in place. Some of the sultan's closest advisors were attempting to convince him that the time had come to abandon the siege. Mehmet did allow some final negotiations regarding terms for the city's surrender. At one point, he offered to allow the city to remain under the emperor's control if Constantine would pay him 100,000 gold bezants (currency) annually. Mehmet knew that the amount would be impossible for the emperor to pay, and it came as no surprise when Constantine turned down the offer. After his advisors spoke for and against the siege, Mehmet sent word to the troops, asking what they preferred. Nearly every one of the Muslim soldiers and sailors made it clear that they wanted to see the siege through to a final victory. Armed with the support of the troops, the sultan finally made up his mind: The siege would continue, and a new assault would soon take place.

Soon, the emperor knew of the sultan's decision. Christian spies in the Turkish camp wrote messages about the Turks' new plans, attached them to arrows, and shot them over the walls of Constantinople.

It was Saturday, May 26. The cannons delivered 1,000-pound (454-kilogram) granite cannonballs with renewed vigor. That night, by the eerie glimmer of flares, the Turks continued their efforts to fill in the Byzantine moat. They brought their guns even closer. The following day, the Mesoteichion section of the wall experienced three direct cannon hits that caused a large part of the wall to tumble down.

As the cannons boomed, the sultan rode his horse through the camp, telling his men that the great assault would soon take place. To give them a new incentive to fight, Mehmet promised that, once they broke Christian resistance and entered the city triumphantly, the troops would get three days to sack the city and take for themselves whatever treasure and valuables they could find. He told them: "by eternal God and His Prophet and by the four thousand prophets and by the souls of his father and his children that all the treasure found in the city would be fairly distributed" among them.

On Sunday, the work of filling the moat continued as thousands worked by torchlight. Everyone in the Turkish camp could feel that the end of the siege was near. They believed the next few days would bring them victory. As they worked, dragging up material to fill the moat, they sang psalms of praise to Allah as Muslim musicians played their trumpets, fifes, and drums. The sultan appeared throughout the evening to offer assurances to his men that the end of the conflict was at hand.

The next day was nearly cloudless. The sun shone

brightly from morning through afternoon. Late in the day, the Muslims used the clear skies to their advantage. As the brilliant sunset blazed in the evening sky, the light nearly blinded the defenders stationed along the wall of the city. Unable to see the Turks through the bright orange sunlight, the Christian knights were unable to respond as the besiegers rushed up to the walls and finished filling in the moat. Meanwhile, other Muslim fighters dragged cannons and siege machines closer than ever to the city walls. Then, as the sun lowered to the horizon, the sky immediately clouded over and a heavy rainstorm began.

Inside the city, the Christian defenders prayed for a miracle. They knew the great attack was coming soon. At one point, some people in the city thought the Turks' camp had burst into flames. Anxious and hopeful citizens scurried to the city's walls to get a look. Their elation did not last. The bright flash was only the Muslim torches lighting up the night skies for the sultan's busy workmen, who were making their way ever closer to the city.

At midnight, the sultan ordered all work to stop. He set aside Monday, May 28, as a day of rest, prayer, worship, and meditation. He planned the assault for the following day. The sultan sent messages to the people of Pera, reminding them of their neutrality and warning them not to aid the Byzantines. He made constant contact with his men, riding up and down the land wall to rally the troops for the coming attack. He rode on the pontoon bridge across the Golden Horn and paid a call to Admiral Hamza Bey. Mehmet instructed the admiral to make ready for the battle the next day. Bey was to cover the possible seaward retreat of the enemy by spreading his ships along the entire length of the walls of Constantinople that touched the coast of the Sea of

Marmara. The sailors were to be equipped with scaling ladders that they might be able to use to breach the seawalls. There was to be no escape for the people trapped inside the city.

Compared to earlier days of cannon bombardment, Monday was a quiet day of contemplation on both sides of the walls of Constantinople. Within the city, the silence was broken by the clanging of church bells. Wall defenders, whether Orthodox and Greek or Catholic and Italian, sang hymns together and begged God for comfort and aid. The emperor moved around the walls, encouraging his men as best he could and praising their efforts of the past seven weeks.

Although the defenders of the city had little left to rely on, they continued, even as the end neared, to hope for a miracle. Desperate for divine help, the people of the city took relics and other holy objects from all the city's great Christian churches and paraded them through the streets of Constantinople. They carried pictures of the Virgin Mary to the city walls. Near the spots where the walls had been heavily damaged, the people asked for the blessings of the mother of Jesus Christ. Even the emperor took part in one of these religious processions.

Later on Monday, crowds of Christians began to meet to pray in the city's churches. People made confessions and took the bread and wine of Communion. Thousands of candles cast a golden glow of flickering light throughout the churches, illuminating the splendid mosaics that pictured God, Jesus Christ, the Apostles, and Christian emperors of centuries past. After the Byzantine soldiers went to Communion, they left the churches and took up their positions on the wall. On the evening of May 28, Emperor Constantine, riding an Arab mare, entered the great Byzantine cathedral of the Hagia Sophia and took Communion himself.

Christians met to pray in the city's churches. Treasures of the Byzantine Church, such as this gold-illuminated psalter (prayer book) were in danger of being destroyed or looted if Constantinople fell to the Turks.

Those who were present in the great ancient church heard the final official words of Constantine. Although accounts of his speech vary, he told them first what they already knew: that the final assault of the Muslims was about to take place. He reminded the knights present that it was a noble deed to die for a just cause. Constantine said that a true man dies gloriously when he gives his life for his country or his emperor. On a more personal level, he stated that to die for one's family or faith were equally important reasons. After all, the Muslims, said Constantine, had arrived at the gates of their city to destroy a stronghold of Christianity. His knights, Constantine informed them, must prepare to die for all four—country, emperor, family, and faith.

Knowing the end might be at hand, the emperor spoke of the past glories of the Byzantine Empire. He tried to give the men a sense of honor and pride by reminding his fellow Greeks and their Italian allies that they had descended from noble knights and Roman warriors, the best of both the Greek and Roman worlds. They would be vastly outnumbered during the coming fight, he said, but they should keep their spirits high and be brave and steadfast, and then God would grant them victory. After his speech, Constantine approached each knight—Greek and Italian alike—and spoke to each, asking forgiveness if he had sinned against any of them. Each man returned the gesture and turned to his fellow knights as well, to ask forgiveness and to embrace each other as doomed comrades. To the last man, each soldier vowed that he was willing to surrender his life for the sake of the emperor and the city.

Just after midnight, the emperor and the knights left the Hagia Sophia for the last time. They bolted the doors of the dome-capped sanctuary behind them, leaving the entire court of Byzantium inside. Constantine then made his way to the walls and took up his position along the Mesoteichion section. He ordered the gates of the wall locked from within the city, behind the defenders, so that no man on the wall could possibly retreat from the bloody battle that lay ahead.

The Battle for
the City Begins

The siege of Constantinople, seen in this detail from a dramatic sixteenth-century wall painting, would change the balance of power between Christian and Muslim forces in Europe and Asia.

The emperor and his knights did not have to wait long. Within an hour, Turkish trumpets and drums sounded amid the battle cries of the Muslim encampments. Church bells within the city pealed in response. Every available man of fighting age was called to the city walls. Even women—including nuns—were pressed into duty to carry water to the defenders. Panic and tears spread from one end of the city to the other. Older people and children took refuge in their houses and in churches. Near the Golden Horn seawall, people crowded into the Church of Saint Theodosia. It was decorated with hundreds of celebration roses. Tuesday, May 29, was the saint's feast day.

Historian Steven Runciman described the unfolding drama of the final day of the Byzantine Empire:

> The sudden noise was horrifying. All along the line of the walls the Turks rushed in to the attack, screaming their battle-cries, while drums and trumpets and fifes urged them on. The Christian troops had been waiting silently; but when the watchmen on the towers gave the alarm the churches near the walls began to ring their bells, and church after church throughout the city took up the warning sound till every belfry was clanging. Three miles away, in the Church of the Holy Wisdom [the Hagia Sophia] the worshippers knew that the battle had begun.

The defenders along the walls now faced an onslaught of Turkish warriors, who came in waves. The first group to fight was made up of the troops known as the Bashi-bazouks. They were soldiers of fortune, Muslim and Christian alike, who had come from all across Europe and Asia to fight. They were an odd assortment of men, and they were not the most skilled members of the sultan's ranks. As mercenaries, they carried a mixed collection of weapons, including bows and arrows, stone-throwing slings, wide-bladed scimitars, and primitive muskets called arquebuses. The sultan sent thousands of them into the fray first, simply to soften up and wear down the enemy. As some Bashi-bazouks turned and fled from the battle, they were met by the sultan's military police who, when necessary, bullied and threatened the Bashi-bazouks to make them go back into the fight. When threats did not work, the military troops struck the fleeing Bashi-bazouks with heavy rods and lashed at them with whips. Behind these enforcers came the sultan's best fighters, the Janissaries, who had orders to hack to death any deserters who tried to leave the battle.

The Bashi-bazouks met stiff resistance as they faced skilled Italian and Greek knights who carried better weapons and wore superior armor. The Bashi-bazouks had another problem, too. There were so many of them that they kept bumping into and stepping on each other as they crowded together along the wall. They were only able to push the assault forward at the area of the city walls adjacent to the Lycus River. Armed with their scaling ladders, the Bashi-bazouks were slaughtered by the dozens as thousands of missiles, rocks, and arrows were fired toward them. Wall defenders dropped boulders, killing three and four Bashi-bazouks at a time. Many of the sultan's soldiers who managed to scale their ladders were killed when they reached the top. After two hours of fighting, the Bashi-bazouks were exhausted and had to surrender. With only minutes between assaults, the tired Christians drank some water, then turned immediately to face the next wave of the enemy: the Anatolian Turks.

These troops were from Asia Minor, and they served as regular cavalry militia. Unlike the Bashi-bazouks, they were highly-trained warriors and skilled horsemen. The Anatolian Turks rode their horses forward in extended lines and dismounted in front of the Mesoteichion portion of the wall, where the Bashi-bazouks had made some headway. All of them were Muslims, ready to die for their sultan and Allah.

They attacked in large numbers just south of where the Bashi-bazouks had massed, at a place called the Gate of St. Romanus. As they rushed toward the wall, Turkish cannons fired and the drummers and trumpeters blared loud martial music. Flares lit up the night sky that hung heavy with clouds. There was confusion and noise, fierce combat and death, blood and sweat. In the faint light before dawn, Urban's massive cannon lobbed a great cannonball against the Byzantine wall, sending up a cloud of debris and dust that choked both the defenders and attackers. The Turks pressed forward, scaling ladders in hand, and mounted their assault. In the moonlight, amid clouds of blinding dust, the Turks fought the Christian defenders. In the confusion, as they faced ferocious resistance, the Anatolian Turks withdrew in defeat. The weary Christian soldiers took the brief rest to work furiously to repair the damage Urban's cannon had done to the wall.

At the same time, other Muslim attackers were besieging the city walls elsewhere. South of the Mesoteichion, the Turks struck at the city's Third Military Gate, but the assault was repulsed. Unlike the walls near the Lycus River, this portion had not been damaged at all. However, the fight at the Third Gate kept several defenders busy and made it difficult for them to help their comrades to the north.

While full-scale assaults created hotspots along the city's perimeter walls, small bands of the sultan's troops were quietly approaching the wall amid the shadows of the night. One by one, they tried to scale their ladders silently so they could gain access to the interior of the city. Their hope was to catch some distracted wall defenders by surprise. Along the seawalls, Turkish sailors also landed and sent out raiding parties. Although all these assaults failed, they did manage to keep the Christian troops on constant alert, regardless of their positions on the wall.

After the attack of the Anatolian Turks along the Mesoteichion, the sultan wasted no time sending in the third wave of attackers. It was the hour of the Janissaries. With great precision, skill, and commitment, the

Janissaries threw themselves into the battle. They approached the wall in perfect columns to face defenders who had just spent most of the night fighting. The elite Muslim troops launched everything they had available at their Christian opponents: spears, lances, stones, arrows, and arquebus bullets. The Janissaries even swung their great scimitars in the hand-to-hand fighting.

Then, someone in the Christian camp made a tragic mistake. Near the Blachernae wall, in the midst of the battle, the Christian soldiers had opened up a small, nearly forgotten sally port called the Kerkoporta. The

A Turkish Prince Helps Defend Constantinople

In general terms, the siege of Constantinople pitted Muslim warriors against the city's Christian defenders. However, these religious lines were not exact. Some of the forces of the sultan were, in fact, Christian mercenaries Mehmet had hired from Germany, Italy, and Hungary. Some were even Greeks. By the same token, during the siege, Emperor Constantine got help from a Turkish prince named Orhan, who had lived in the city almost all his life. When Mehmet became the sultan after his father's death, Orhan was the only other Ottoman prince in line for the throne. Having been exiled to Constantinople as a small boy, Orhan and his fellow Turks gave their loyalty to Constantine when the siege began. Orhan and his men were placed along the seawalls to defend a site near the mouth of the Lycus River.

When the final assault on the city began on May 29, Orhan and his Turkish fighters defended their portion of the wall with vigor. He and his men knew what would happen to them if they were taken prisoner by the forces of the sultan. When a Turkish victory seemed certain, Orhan tried to escape by dressing in the robes of a Greek monk. Since he spoke Greek fluently, his disguise just might have worked. After capture, though, a fellow Turk betrayed him, revealing the renegade prince's true identity. As punishment for his treason against his fellow Ottomans, Orhan's head was chopped off on the spot.

The battle for Constantinople was more than a fight for territory and power. It was viewed by both Christian and Muslim warriors as a religious struggle —and both sides hoped that God was on their side.

purpose of this kind of opening was to let wall defenders slip outside the wall during a battle so they could carry out a hit-and-run attack against the enemy, then return back inside the safety of the wall. After troops came back from one such hasty assault, the door was accidentally left open. The Turks soon realized the error and rushed their own men into the city through the small opening. Dozens of Turks filled the area behind the wall and began to climb up a stairway to the top of the rampart. Christian soldiers drove many of them back through the open sally port, then closed the opening behind them.

Unknown to the Byzantines, however, in the confusion of battle, nearly 50 Turks were left inside the city walls.

At about the same time, another setback occurred for the Christians. A ball pierced the chest armor of the leader of the Genoese knights, the great commander Giustiniani, wounding him severely. It was he who had brought 700 Genoese to aid the city before the siege had begun. He had been appointed commander of the defense of Constantinople by the emperor. He had faced repeated assaults by the Turks at the Mesoteichion section of the wall over the past seven weeks. He provided valiant leadership in defense of the city. Now he was bleeding heavily and asked to be taken from the wall. Constantine rushed to his side and begged him not to leave his post. Giustiniani was a broken man, however. He had had enough of the fight and believed the battle was lost.

Because the wall doors had been locked before the battle, the Genoese soldiers had to open a small gate before they could carry the wounded Giustiniani into the city. As their commander left the wall, many of his men decided to go with him. They feared the battle was over and the Turks were at hand. Then, the Turks who had stayed within the city after the closing of the sally port were spotted. Panic ensued. Genoese soldiers shouted that the Turks were in the city, and fled through the newly opened gate. Confusion and fear spread along the wall, and Mehmet, watching from the battlefield, saw an opportunity for his men. He ordered the Janissaries to make another assault, shouting: "The city is ours!"

Led by a towering soldier named Hasan, the Janissaries fought with renewed vigor. He and dozens of his fellow warriors swung their scimitars wildly, cutting down Christian defenders, while also managing to break through the rubble and barrels of the breached wall.

Others followed them. Even after Hasan was killed, the Janissaries continued to stream through the wall, their numbers too great for the defenders of Constantinople. Once inside, the Turks moved to the inner wall and took it over while they fought off the dwindling opposition. A Turkish soldier raised a flag from a defense tower. This caused the Muslims outside to rally in excitement. Other flags were hoisted as the followers of Islam spread out along the city walls.

When the emperor received word of the breach, he and three of his officers raced on horseback to the occupied point along the wall. Constantine's colleagues included a loyal Spanish soldier, a cousin, and one of his most trusted officers. All of them tried one last time to reorganize the panicky Christian troops, but it was too late. The four men realized that the end was near. They also knew they would soon face certain death if they did not flee from their positions on the wall. Even so, the four resolved to keep fighting rather than live with the disgrace of having lost Byzantium. Constantine's cousin was the first to move as he shouted and ran headlong into a horde of enemy troops. The others soon followed, including the emperor. Before he entered the battle in those final minutes, Constantine removed any official insignia that would indicate to the Turks that he was the emperor. Then, he fought his way into a crowd of Janissaries, never to be seen again.

The city fell apart almost at once. More and more Turks entered the city through breaks in the wall, while Turkish ships in the Horn landed sailors ready to fight along the seawalls. The people of the city evacuated their homes and ran through the streets in terror. Others simply surrendered, pleading with the Turks not to destroy their homes. Venetian and Genoese ships, filled with defeated soldiers and refugees who feared for their lives, attempted to slip away from the lost city. The great chain across the Golden Horn was hacked from its moorings, which opened up the channel for escape. The Muslim navy captured several of the ships, although the others were able to sail to safety. By noon on May 29, the city, harbor, and more than a dozen Christian ships were in the hands of the sultan's forces. Constantinople was vanquished. Sultan Mehmet now held within his grasp the last remnant of the once-glorious Roman Empire.

Sacking the
Ancient City

When the Turks finally broke through the city's defenses, they entered Constantinople and began to slaughter both soldiers and citizens. They also pillaged the city's valuables and even desecrated ancient Christian churches.

erhaps the worst was yet to come. The Turks soon set out to destroy the ancient city of Constantinople. The sultan had promised them three days during which they could loot every corner of the capital. Since Constantine had refused to surrender the city, Islamic law offered no protection to the city's occupants or possessions. Highly charged Turkish soldiers and sailors seemed to go wild. They ran through the streets, killing anyone who seemed to be fleeing, even small children. Streams of blood flowed through the streets of Constantinople. Conservative estimates put the number of people killed that day at 4,000.

Nothing was safe from the Muslim invaders. They ransacked homes and stole everything that they thought had any value at all.

They raided the royal palace, as well as churches and libraries. Thousands of ancient books, including Bibles and other religious works, were seized. The precious stones were ripped from their adorned covers, and then the books were thrown into fires. Men attacked buildings, removing golden and jeweled items. They even hacked away at ornamental marble to take pieces for themselves. Holy items, including icons of the Virgin Mary, were burned or chopped into kindling. After Muslim soldiers had plundered a building or home, they left a small flag at the door as a sign to inform other looters that the place had already been sacked.

Although the Turks at first slew Christian refugees in the streets, they soon realized that many of their victims were worth more alive than dead. Women were captured to be sold as slaves. Many who resisted were hacked to death. Those who went along were stripped naked and humiliated, even raped. Turkish soldiers took the women's brightly colored scarves and bound their wrists together to form a long chain of human captives. As the Turks invaded holy places such as monasteries and nunneries, their occupants were enslaved, too. Some nuns refused to give in to their captors. They chose instead to commit suicide by leaping into deep water wells. In all, the Turks may have enslaved as many as 20,000 residents of the city of Constantinople.

Those who had taken refuge the night before the final battle in the Hagia Sophia soon fell into the hands of the Muslim victors. Turks battered down the barred doors of the cathedral. Noblewomen were enslaved and the elderly slaughtered. The Muslims then grabbed any religious items of value. Some of the Muslims began to tear the building up, destroying mosaics and marbles.

Most of the several thousand Christian soldiers and knights who had defended the city for seven exhausting weeks had been killed already. Even as the Turks invaded the city streets in search of the spoils of war, however, some defenders had not yet surrendered. A small company of sailors from the Mediterranean island of Crete continued to fight, as they held three towers along the entrance of the Golden Horn. They stood their ground until the early afternoon. After their surrender, the Turks, who were so impressed with their bravery, allowed them to go free.

On the afternoon of May 29, Mehmet rode into Constantinople on horseback. Historian Ralph Vickers described the procession of the Muslim victor:

> The Sultan . . . made his own triumphal entry into Constantinople that afternoon. The great domes and spires still stood unscathed, but by now the buildings were shorn of their wealth and beauty. The streets were abandoned. Leading a procession of his guards, chief commanders and ministers, he toured the central portions of the city he had conquered. At the hippodrome he came across the twisted columns of the three serpents. In his eyes this was a [great symbol] of the city. In a test of strength with the iron mace he still carried he shattered one of the huge jaws.

Mehmet made his way without hesitation to the Hagia Sophia to see the ancient church for himself. As he dismounted near the cathedral's massive gates, he scooped up some dirt, filtering it through his fingers and onto his turbaned head. After making this pious act, the sultan entered the Hagia Sophia. Immediately, he was awed at the building's splendor. Near the altar, he scolded one of his men, who was trying to break loose a marble slab. He warned the Turk to stop what he was doing, explaining that they were in a house of God. The sultan then announced to his men that the few Christians who were still hiding in the shadows should not be harmed. The sultan was so inspired by the wonders of the Church of the Divine Wisdom that he declared that the shrine would be turned into a temple to Allah that very day. The 1,000-year-old Hagia Sophia was to become the Mosque (Islamic house of worship) of the Divine Wisdom. Before he left the sacred edifice, the sultan dropped to his knees to recite prayers, with his turbaned head bent to touch the great church's marble floor in humility.

Despite his promise of three days of pillaging, the sultan ordered the violence to stop after only one day. Mehmet even sent his own military police into the streets of the city to restore order. Then he had all the spoils of war brought before him and redistributed the prizes, making certain that those who had been unable to take part in the looting would receive a fair share of the city's wealth.

Despite the restoration of peace in the streets of Constantinople, all was not calm just yet. Seeking revenge against those Italians who had attempted to help the Byzantines defend their capital, the sultan ordered many to be executed. He then selected 1,200 captive Byzantine children to be enslaved and sent 400 to each of three fellow Muslim rulers: the sultan of Egypt and the kings of Tunis and Grenada.

Mehmet himself remained in Constantinople for three weeks. When he finally set out to return to his royal palace in Adrianople, the Christian capital was in ruins. Fire had destroyed many of its buildings, while other structures were ruined by pillage and desecration. Monasteries, churches, homes, shops, and public buildings were empty, and often blackened, shells. As he rode out of the city, the sultan was moved to weep for Constantinople. He whispered softly: "What a city we have given over to plunder and destruction."

Just 11 days after the fall of Constantinople, word of the great Byzantine capital's collapse began to make its way to

Although the sultan spared many Christians whom his troops attempted to kill, he did allow the execution of the Italians who had helped defend the Byzantine capital.

Europe. On June 9, three shiploads of Cretan sailors, who had been among the last to surrender to the Turks, arrived in their home island's port of Candia. They told the news of the loss of the Christian capital of the East. The people of Crete were shocked, unable to imagine the collapse of the great city. One monk wrote: "There has never been and there never will be a more dreadful happening."

Soon, all of Europe was aware that Constantinople had fallen into the hands of the Turks. For many, it was inconceivable. Legends had been told about the city's invincibility. Everyone knew of the immense and elaborate walls that had protected the city for 1,000 years. Those who might have been able to provide aid to the city— the Venetians, the pope, other Western leaders—had misjudged the old city's ability to stand in the face of a vast Turkish army. Ironically, several Venetian ships had in fact been fitted to sail to aid of Constantinople, but they had remained docked on the Aegean Sea island of Chios while they waited for good winds. The favorable winds—and the much-needed aid—never came.

Even after its fall, the city of Constantinople, despite its occupation by Turkish Muslims, did not fade into history, lost in ruin and rubble. Several buildings, including major churches, even managed to survive the destructive rampage of the Muslims. The Hagia Sophia was desecrated, but the second largest church in the city, the Cathedral of the Holy Apostles, survived, probably after the sultan ordered its preservation, just as he had the Church of the Divine Wisdom. May 29, 1453, marked the end of Constantinople as the head of the Christian Empire in the East, but the sultan allowed its Greek residents to stay in the city to live as his subjects. He even granted them freedom to worship in the Orthodox Church. In fact, he declared the church's patriarch (religious head) as the leader of the Greeks in the city, allowing them to operate as a Christian community within an otherwise Muslim world. Christians, however, would always remain a minority in the city after Muslim control was established. Over the centuries, many Christian churches were refashioned into mosques. By the 1800s, only three Byzantine-era churches remained as Christian houses of worship.

As for the neighboring Genoa-controlled city of Pera, it was forced to accept Islamic rule. Just five days after the collapse of the Byzantine capital, Mehmet visited Pera. He ordered the destruction of the city-colony's land walls and had his troops collect all the weapons held by the people in the city. Mehmet put a Turkish governor to rule over the city. Now the mighty sultan of the Ottoman Empire controlled both sides of the entrance into the Golden Horn. Like ripples across the waters, the fall of the Genoan city led to the ultimate collapse of other Genoan trading outposts farther east in the Crimean Sea.

For his part, Mehmet's plans for Constantinople continued for nearly 30 years after his successful siege. In the wake of the wholesale destruction of the city by his own men, and given the fact that the city had declined over the prior several centuries, the sultan worked hard to rebuild Constantinople as a magnificent urban center, but he did it in Muslim style. Mehmet built a palace within the city's walls. He saw himself as the inheritor of the Eastern Roman Empire. He invited Byzantine families who had fled the city as Muslim invaders entered to return and take up residence once again, now under his protection. He also invited Turks to live in Constantinople, and gave them assistance to build homes or to open up businesses.

For the next 470 years, from 1453 to 1922, Constantinople served as the capital of the Ottoman Empire until its collapse during World War I. Then, in 1923, the Turkish Republic was formed out of the ashes of the old Islamic empire. At that time, the Turks founded a new capital, Ankara. Still, Constantinople—known to the Turks after 1453 as Istanbul—remained the most important Turkish-controlled city, a leading center of business, shipping, trade, and culture.

With Mehmet's victory, the ancient city took on another life, one that was more cosmopolitan and complex, with former enemies living together within the same ancient walls. A generation after the siege, the city experienced a four-fold increase in population. By the mid-1500s, Constantinople was home to more than 500,000 people. The Christian era of the city, established by the first Roman emperor named Constantine, had come to an end. In the future, the city would be a place where people of different faiths would live, sharing the present yet ever mindful of the past.

The Later Years of "Mehmet the Conqueror"

The victory of Sultan Mehmet over Constantinople would prove to be the crowning achievement of his lengthy reign. It was certainly not his final military campaign, though. For the next 30 years, Mehmet found himself fighting someone somewhere almost constantly. Most of his campaigns of conquest ended with his winning more lands for his vast Islamic kingdom. He and his huge armies marched into various corners of both Asia and Europe, dethroning rulers and putting many to death. Military ventures led by Mehmet in Bosnia, the Crimea, Albania, the province of Cappadocia, various Greek islands, and parts of Hungary all met with success. At one point in his conquests, his armies nearly arrived at the outskirts of the great Italian city-state of Venice itself.

Only two of Mehmet's major campaigns failed: an attempt to seize the city of Belgrade in 1456, and a war against the Mediterranean island of Rhodes in 1480. The Belgrade siege was a painful loss for Mehmet. Although he had raised an army of 150,000 men and brought along 300 cannons, he met stiff resistance. Western European powers may have failed to come to the rescue of Constantinople in 1453, but they rallied behind the people of Belgrade. In one battle, the Hungarians drove the Turks back, captured many of their cannons, and even wounded Mehmet himself. The campaign ended with a loss of 50,000 of the sultan's warriors.

Mehmet died at the age of 51, just as he was raising an army for yet another campaign. Since he had told no one where he intended to fight next, his goal died with him. The great sultan of the vast lands of the Ottoman Empire was buried in the city he had conquered in 1453, the first of his many military conquests: Constantinople.

Even today, centuries after the siege of Constantinople, Turks still celebrate the fall of the Byzantine Empire, which helped pave the way for the creation of modern Turkey.

A.D. 324	Roman Emperor Constantine the Great moves the eastern Roman capital to the city of Byzantium; the city becomes the capital of the later Byzantine Empire.
330	Constantine renames Byzantium Constantinople after himself.
537	Byzantine Emperor Justinian the Great completes initial building of the great church, the Hagia Sophia, or the Church of the Divine Wisdom.
500s	Justinian greatly expands the borders of the Byzantine Empire.
600	The Prophet Muhammad founds the religion of Islam.
670s	Islamic armies lay siege to Constantinople without success.
711	Islamic armies have reduced the size of the Byzantine Empire.
717	Islamic armies lay siege to Constantinople, again without success.
800	Western Frankish King Charlemagne is crowned emperor of the Roman Empire; Byzantium is reduced to the status of a Greek empire.

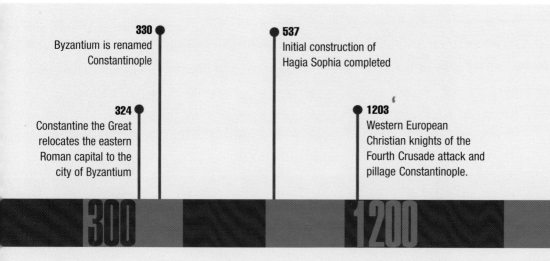

330
Byzantium is renamed
Constantinople

537
Initial construction of
Hagia Sophia completed

324
Constantine the Great
relocates the eastern
Roman capital to the
city of Byzantium

1203
Western European
Christian knights of the
Fourth Crusade attack and
pillage Constantinople.

300

1200

Timeline

867–1056	Fortunes of Constantinople turn around as the empire experiences prosperity; during the reign of Byzantine Emperor Basil II, the empire annexes many new lands.
1000s	Byzantium faces invasions by two forces: the Muslims in the East and the Normans, or Vikings, in the West.
1203	Western European Christian knights, bound for the Holy Land on the Fourth Crusade, attack and pillage the city of Constantinople.
1100s	Constantinople generally remains a wealthy and dazzling city, but its political power has begun to decline.
1347	Black Death strikes the Byzantine Empire, killing as many as two out of every three people.
1402	Turkish Muslims lay siege to the city of Constantinople; again, they fail.
1422	The Turkish Muslims, under a new sultan, once again lay siege to Constantinople; but a rebellion in the Ottoman Empire brings the siege to an abrupt end.

1451
Nineteen-year-old Sultan Mehmet II comes to power over the Turkish Empire.

1449
Byzantine Emperor Constantine XI takes the throne.

May 29, 1453
The Turks launch an all-out assault on the Constantinople. The city collapses.

1453–1922
Constantinople (renamed Istanbul) serves as the capital of the Ottoman Empire.

1923
Turkish republic is formed and the new capital established at Ankara.

1450   **1950**

1452–1453
Sultan Mehmet raises an army for the siege of Constantinople.

April 22, 1453
Turks haul ships overland from the Bosporus to the Golden Horn.

April 5–6, 1453
Sultan Mehmet arrives on the outskirts of the city of Constantinople.

1430	Turks manage to capture the Byzantine city of Thessalonica, one of the last of the major Byzantine urban centers.
1449	Byzantine Emperor Constantine XI takes the throne.
1451	Nineteen-year-old Sultan Mehmet II comes to power over the Turkish Empire.
1452	Mehmet builds castle along the banks of the Bosporus, putting him in close proximity to Constantinople; castle is completed in August.
Fall 1452–Spring 1453	Mehmet raises an army for the siege of Constantinople.

1453:

January	Mehmet hires Hungarian armament maker Urban to build a huge cannon for the coming siege; within the city, Genoan leader Giovanni Longo Giustiniani offers his services to the emperor.
March	Urban's monstrous cannon arrives near Constantinople.
April 5	Mehmet arrives on the outskirts of the city.
April 6	Turkish warriors take up positions to begin the siege of the city.
April 12	Turks have established 14 batteries of cannons, each of which has four guns aimed at Constantinople and its extensive defense walls.
April 18	Mehmet orders a night assault against Constantinople's Fifth Military Gate; Janissaries lead the assault and are repelled.
April 20	Christian ships from Genoa, sent by the pope, defeat the Turks in an intense sea battle in the Sea of Marmara; the Turks lose several ships, and suffer 400 casualties, including 100 deaths.
April 22	Turks haul ships overland from the Bosporus to the Golden Horn.
April 28	Christian knights launch a night raid on Turkish ships in the Golden Horn; the raid is a failure.
May 3	Rescue mission launched by forces of the emperor; ships are dispatched, disguised as Turkish vessels, to find much-needed food and military aid from European leaders.
May 6	Urban's cannon, after having been out of commission, is fully operational again and begins to pound the city's walls.
May 12	Muslim land forces launch a night attack along the portion of the defense wall called Blachernae, but fail to break through the city's complicated wall system.
May 18	Turks use a siege tower to approach the city walls, but Christian knights sneak out of the city that night and blow it up.

May 23	Rescue ships return, having failed in their mission to find food and Western support.
May 24	An eclipse darkens the sky above Constantinople; Christians in the city see the event as a bad sign.
May 25	Heavy fog shrouds the city; the Christians interpret the fog as a sign of disaster.
May 26	Turkish cannons launch 1,000-pound (454-kilogram) granite cannonballs; that night, the Turks resume their efforts to fill in the moat in front of the city's land walls.
May 27	Thousands of Turkish workers have managed to fill in the moat.
May 28	Sultan sets aside the day for rest and prayers; within the city, Christians also pray for their deliverance; that evening, Constantine enters the Church of the Divine Wisdom to take his last Communion; then, he and his officers man the city walls for the coming attack.
May 29	Between 1:00 A.M. and 2:00 A.M., the Turks launch an all-out assault on the city; the fighting is intense and furious, but the Turks breach the walls of Constantinople; Christian knights abandon the city; the people panic as the Turks begin to rampage and plunder the Christian capital; the Genoan Giustiniani is wounded and abandons the fight; during the fighting, the emperor is killed; the city of Constantinople collapses; that afternoon, the sultan enters the city on horseback and pays a visit to the Church of the Divine Wisdom.
1453–1922	Constantinople (renamed Istanbul) serves as the capital of the Ottoman Empire.
1483	Mehmet II dies.
1923	Turkish republic is formed and the new capital established at Ankara; even to the present, Constantinople (Istanbul) remains Turkey's most important center of business, shipping, trade, and culture.

CHAPTER 3, THE SULTAN SETS THE STAGE

Page 30: "Only one thing I want . . ." Steven Runciman, *The Fall of Constantinople*. London: Cambridge University Press, 1966, p. 74.

CHAPTER 4, THE BATTLE UNFOLDS

Page 43: "Artillery was still primitive . . ." Ralph Vickers, "The Siege of Constantinople: Preparation." (*http://www.geocities.com/Athens/Academy/5 990/byzantine/byzantine03.html*)

Page 49: "Mehmet returned to his tent . . ." Ibid.

CHAPTER 5, A BELEAGUERED CITY

Page 57: "Since the great cannon fused . . ." Nestor-Iskander, *The Tale of Constantinople*. New Rochelle, NY: Aristide D. Caratzas, Publisher, 1998, p. 53.

Page 57: "As evening had already set . . ." Ibid., p. 55.

Page 61: "And in the company . . ." Ibid., p. 65.

Page 62: "by eternal God and His Prophet . . ." Steven Runciman, *The Fall of Constantinople*. London: Cambridge University Press, 1966, p. 126.

CHAPTER 6, THE BATTLE FOR THE CITY BEGINS

Page 70: "The sudden noise was horrifying . . ." Steven Runciman, *The Fall of Constantinople*. London: Cambridge University Press, 1966, p. 133.

Page 75: "The city is ours! . . ." Ibid., p. 138.

CHAPTER 7, SACKING THE ANCIENT CITY

Page 81: "The Sultan . . . made his own . . ." Ralph Vickers, "The Siege of Constantinople: Pillage and Procession." (*http://www.geocities.com/Athens/Academy/5 990/byzantine/byzantine11.html*)

Page 82: "What a city we have given . . ." Steven Runciman, *The Fall of Constantinople*. London: Cambridge University Press, 1966, p. 152.

Page 83: "There has never been and there . . ." Ibid., p. 160.

Eversley, Lord. *The Turkish Empire: Its Growth and Decay*. New York: Dodd, Mead and Company, 1917.

Fox, Edward Whiting, ed. *Atlas of European History*. New York: Oxford University Press, 1964.

Intalcik, Halil. *The Ottoman Empire: The Classical Age 1300–1600*. New York: Praeger Publishers, 1973.

Krautheimer, Richard. *Early Christian and Byzantine Architecture*. New York: Penguin, 1965.

Nestor-Iskander. *The Tale of Constantinople (of Its Origin and Capture by the Turks in the Year 1453)*, trans. Walter K. Hanak and Marios Philippides. New Rochelle, NY: Aristide D. Caratzas, Publisher, 1998.

Runciman, Steven. *Byzantine Civilisation*. London: Edward Arnold (Publishers) Ltd., 1966.

———. *The Fall of Constantinople, 1453*. London: Cambridge University Press, 1965.

Sherrard, Philip. *Byzantium*. (Great Ages of Man: A History of the World's Cultures) New York: TIME-Life Books, 1966.

Toy, Sidney. *A History of Fortification from 3000 B.C. to A.D. 1700*. London: William Heinemann, Ltd., 1955.

Van Millingen, Alexander. *Byzantine Constantinople: The Walls of the City and Adjoining Historical Sites*. London: John Murray, Albermarle Street, 1899.

Zernov, Nicolas. *Eastern Christendom: A Study and Development of the Eastern Orthodox Church*. New York: G. P. Putnam, 1961.

Asimov, Isaac. *Constantinople: The Forgotten Empire*. Boston: Houghton Mifflin Company, 1970.

Corrick, James. *The Byzantine Empire*. San Diego: Lucent Books, 1997.

Leacroft, Helen. *Buildings of Byzantium*. Boston: Addison Wesley Longman, 1977.

Sherrard, Philip. *Byzantium*. Silver, Burdett & Ginn, 1966.

TIM MCNEESE is an Associate Professor of History at York College in Nebraska. Professor McNeese earned an Associate of Arts degree from York College, a Bachelor of Arts degree in history and political science from Harding University, and a Master of Arts degree in history from Southwest Missouri State Univeristy. He is currently in his 27th year of teaching.

Professor McNeese's writing career has earned him a citation in the "Something About the Author" reference work. He is the author of more than fifty books and educational materials on everything from Egyptian pyramids to American Indians. He is married to Beverly McNeese, who teaches English at York College.